20 MILLIONAI₹E$ UNDER 30

Sophia Graham writes books simply because she loves good stories. Having been an editor who has spent over a decade working with major publishing houses of the world and with award-winning authors, stories are her life and her bread and butter. She believes that the greatest stories are the ones that emerge from the lives of people around us. Sophia has also taught editing, and many of her students have now gone on to become storytellers and story makers themselves. When she is not writing books for adults, she writes English textbooks for school children. Sophia resides in the US with her husband and a lifetime collection of books.

20 MILLIONAI₹E$ UNDER 30

SOPHIA GRAHAM

RUPA

Published by
Rupa Publications India Pvt. Ltd 2021
7/16, Ansari Road, Daryaganj
New Delhi 110002

Sales Centres:
Allahabad Bengaluru Chennai
Hyderabad Jaipur Kathmandu
Kolkata Mumbai

Copyright © Sohini Ghose 2021

The views and opinions expressed in this book are the author's own and the facts are as reported by her which have been verified to the extent possible, and the publishers are not in any way liable for the same.

All rights reserved.

No part of this publication may be reproduced, transmitted, or stored in a retrieval system, in any form or by any means, electronic, mechanical, photocopying, recording or otherwise, without the prior permission of the publisher.

ISBN: 978-93-90918-32-4

First impression 2021

10 9 8 7 6 5 4 3 2 1

The moral right of the author has been asserted.

Printed at Thomson Press India Ltd., Faridabad

This book is sold subject to the condition that it shall not, by way of trade or otherwise, be lent, resold, hired out, or otherwise circulated, without the publisher's prior consent, in any form of binding or cover other than that in which it is published.

*To the dreamers of yesterday
who make it possible for us to dream today.*

CONTENTS

Introduction		*ix*
1.	TURNING THE TABLES *Akshay Ruparelia: Founder of Doorsteps*	1
2.	THE POWER OF FAILURE *Bhavish Aggarwal: Founder of Ola*	8
3.	SETTING THE RULES *Bill Gates: Co-founder of Microsoft and Gates Foundation*	16
4.	WORK IS PLAY, PLAY IS WORK *Blake Ross: Co-founder of Firefox*	25
5.	DESIGNING DREAMS *Brian Chesky: Co-founder of Airbnb*	33
6.	STARTING A REVOLUTION *Chad Hurley: Co-founder of YouTube*	43
7.	SOLVING PROBLEMS *Drew Houston: Co-founder of Dropbox*	52
8.	REACHING FOR THE STARS *Elon Musk: Co-founder of PayPal, Founder of Tesla and SpaceX*	60
9.	DARING TO BE DIFFERENT *Evan Spiegel: Founder of Snapchat*	69

10.	IMAGINING THE IMPOSSIBLE *Larry Page: Co-founder of Google*	77
11.	HUSTLING FOR HAPPINESS *Lilly Singh: YouTuber, Author,* *Host of* A Little Late with Lilly Singh	86
12.	CONNECTING THE WORLD *Mark Zuckerberg: Co-founder of Facebook*	95
13.	INNOVATING TECHNOLOGY *Patrick Collison: Co-founder of Stripe*	105
14.	BREAKING NEW GROUND *Pierre Omidyar: Founder of eBay*	114
15.	CHALLENGING CONVENTIONS *Richard Branson: Founder of the* *Virgin Group of Companies*	122
16.	TREADING NEW GROUND *Sabeer Bhatia: Founder of Hotmail*	132
17.	DARING TO BE DIFFERENT *Sara Blakely: Founder of Spanx*	140
18.	THE POWER OF PASSION *Steve Ballmer: CEO at Microsoft*	149
19.	TURNING OPPOSITION INTO OPPORTUNITY *Varun Agarwal: Author; Filmmaker;* *Founder of Last Minute Films, Alma Mater,* *Grades Don't Matter*	158
20.	KEEPING IT SIMPLE *Warren Buffett: Founder of Berkshire Hathaway*	166
Conclusion		175

INTRODUCTION

The only source of knowledge is experience.

—ALBERT EINSTEIN

*I am always ready to learn although
I do not always like being taught.*

—WINSTON CHURCHILL

I hate lectures. I hate it even more when people tell me how I should or should not live my life. I find free advice unappetizing and, perhaps for that very reason, I have never taken too well to self-help books. Don't get me wrong: I'm all for learning. It's just that I learn better from experiences rather than instruction. I find that greater lessons are hidden in life stories than we can ever hope to find through mere information gathering. Think back for a second. Humans have been telling stories from time immemorial and most of our lives are spent in telling and retelling stories.

As children, our first lessons came from stories—those that our grandparents and parents told us, those found in *Aesop's Fables*, the *Panchatantra* or the epics, those we read in fairy tales and children's books. These are stories that we pass on to the next generation and the next, and this way, the lessons in these stories—cultural, moral, ethical, social—get passed on too.

Think about it. We humans lead very storied lives. Our lives have a distinct beginning, middle and end, and a narrative that is full of a range of emotions and experiences. We use stories daily to pass along information, share insights, talk about memories or simply give commonsensical advice. We remember and recall better too when information is conveyed to us through stories. For instance, I find myself connecting with strangers, whom I've perhaps met at a party, in the lift, on the plane even more when they share a personal anecdote about their lives with me. It creates an immediate connection and a transformative and empathetic experience, which remains in my memory for much longer.

It has been proven that we learn better from stories than from mere instruction. For instance, if I told a child not to lean over the railing because she might fall and hurt herself, it will leave a lesser impact on her than if I were to tell her the story of a cousin who fell from the second floor of a building and broke her leg. Here, lessons are learnt not through personal experience but through imagining the experience of another person.

The fact that it actually happened to someone makes it all the more tangible and believable. Stories about other people's lives are not only a great tool for teaching us life lessons, but they are also the perfect modes of providing inspiration and hope, making us believe in our own potential and bridging the distance between our dreams and reality. History is replete with those, and every day new stories are being added to its annals.

WHY I WROTE THIS BOOK

The lives of those listed in this book inspired me immensely and I wrote this book in an effort to share that inspiration with all of you. My motivation behind writing this book was to provide hope and encouragement through real-life stories. Self-help books, those that rely heavily on imparting life lessons, often tend to become too didactic. But if we were to learn life lessons, what better way to learn them than from the lives of those who have already walked on the path to success and achievement? This book is a collection of stories and anecdotes from the lives of 20 self-made millionaires who prove that it is possible to become a millionaire before you turn 30. It is not possible for all of us to meet these people and learn about their lives directly from them. But this book can bring you close to them. It can give you a peek into the lives of those who inspire us, who set examples and who are the epitome of success in today's society.

The stories in this book exemplify that the journey to success might not be smooth, but it is an achievable one. It shows that the people in this book are just like any of us. Their lives, too, are full of ups and downs, their journeys are often similar to ours and their dreams and ambitions are as real as ours. With this book, I want to bring you closer to the people you idolize and help you understand them a little more. I want you to see that they are just like you and me in their struggles, in their emotions and in their dreams. After all, only when we relate can we be inspired, and only when we are inspired can we achieve.

WHO THIS BOOK IS FOR

This is a book for all those people who dream of making it big, not only in terms of money but also in life. It is also for those people who encourage others to dream. There are almost 47 million millionaires in the world. And although they may seem a rather small percentage of the 7.8 billion people in the world (and growing every day), it still is a large number.

It is easier to become a millionaire today. With the resources we have at hand, the emergence of social media, the rapid increase in globalization, the thriving entrepreneurial world and the access to information and opportunity, becoming a millionaire at a young age is a realistic possibility today. So, at a time like this, it makes one wonder: if there are so many millionaires in the world, what can I do to become one too? What does it really take to become a millionaire? Does a person need to be born into wealth or can money be earned and acquired? Can it be done before one turns 30? Let's start by deciding that yes, you can become a millionaire. You can become a millionaire before 30 and even after. For the how to, read this book. The lives and life lessons of 20 self-made millionaires will help you find the answers to your questions. Use their lives as a roadmap for yourself. Use their experiences as a blueprint. Use their words as a guide.

USING THIS BOOK

In this book, you will meet 20 millionaires and read about their childhoods, their lives, their education, their principles and, most importantly, their mindsets. You will understand their journey and why and how they became millionaires at such a young age. Contrary to popular belief, their journeys have not always been paved with success. Many of them have failed many times over. But what unites them is that they all kept going. They stumbled but did not stop. They never gave up on their mission.

You can use this book to see your reflection in the lives of the millionaires that are between these pages. You can use this book to relate to the millionaires, to understand that you are not much different from them, to see what changes you can bring into your own life and your attitude to become a millionaire, to find in yourself the potential to achieve anything you want and to realize that becoming a millionaire under 30 is not just a probability for you; it is a possibility.

The prime purpose of this book is to make you see that you are no different from these millionaires, that you have it in you as much as they had it in them to become successful, that the journey to becoming a millionaire isn't necessarily a long one, that you can be young and a millionaire at the same time, that just like the people mentioned in these pages, you too can live the life you want.

Each story in this book is short and interspersed with simple lessons that have emerged from the lives of these people and can make you see what they did to become who they are, which can in turn help you become who you want to be. You will notice that many of the lessons are rather similar. They have common themes of hard work, perseverance and risk-taking running through them. In fact, when you finish reading this book, you can create your own little notebook of one-liner lessons that you might glean from reading about the lives of these millionaires. Keep these lessons handy. Use them as life mottos. Refer to them to inspire yourself.

WHY THIS BOOK IS WHAT YOU NEED

Making money and becoming a millionaire is not an exercise in vanity. It is also not only about earning and accumulating a lot of wealth. Becoming a millionaire is actually about fulfilling your dreams, about realizing your inner potential, about prospering and flourishing in life and about helping others on the way. The people mentioned in this book are millionaires not simply because they made a lot of money but because they dared to dream, followed their passion, overcame their obstacles and accomplished their goals. They are millionaires because they made the seemingly impossible possible.

As I told you at the beginning, I learn best through stories. I hope that the stories of inspiration that you will find in this book will stay with you on your journey to success. I hope that you can draw from the experiences mentioned here and use them in your own lives to chart your own journeys. I hope you can come back to this book, to these stories, again and again, when you are feeling demotivated, when you are feeling stuck or when you simply want to reassure yourself that you can do it. I hope this book makes you believe in yourself and your potential.

Finally, before you turn the page, I want to remind you that this book is not so much about the millionaires mentioned in these pages as it is about you. You are the protagonist of your life story. You are the next millionaire in the making.

Chapter 1

TURNING THE TABLES

Akshay Ruparelia: Founder of Doorsteps

Standing in the middle of the playground at Queen Elizabeth High School in Barnet, London, on a break during his A-level exams, Akshay Ruparelia gets an email on his phone. He has made his first sale—a house with five bedrooms and a swimming pool for £640,000. So happy is Akshay's first client that he calls the 17-year-old Akshay a 'legend, an absolute star'.[1]

The seller, a man from Sussex, had approached Akshay to sell his house for him after stumbling upon Akshay's new website, doorsteps.co.uk, which advertised itself as an online estate agent, charging a fee of only £99 for its services. Excited and nervous for what was to become his first business venture, Akshay enlisted the help of his sister's then boyfriend, whom she later married, Prash Thakrar, to drive him down to the property so that he could take some pictures for the website. Akshay was too young to have a driving license; Prash was paid £40 for his troubles and Akshay got the pictures he

---

[1] Jeremy Armstrong and Hayley Minn, 'Britain's "Youngest Millionaire" Explains How Caring for Sister and Deaf Parents Has Been a Blessing in Disguise', *The Mirror*, 19 October 2017. Available at https://www.mirror.co.uk/tv/tv-news/britains-youngest-millionaire-explains-how-11369579; accessed on 11 March 2021.

needed. Within three weeks of being enlisted, the property was sold! Since Akshay was in the midst of his A levels, he could not celebrate his first sale and had to only make do with Domino's pizza! He did, however, manage to simultaneously set up his business and gain an A+ in Math, A+ in Economics, A in History, A+ in Politics and A in Financial Studies. The satisfied seller went on to use Doorsteps to sell an adjacent property too.

You are never too young to begin your first venture.

Born to an immigrant father of Indian origin, Kaushik, and an Indian-origin British mother, Renuka, Akshay is the younger of two siblings. Akshay and his older sister grew up as carers for their parents who are both deaf. Protecting his parents, being their voice and taking part in important decision-making processes for the family instilled in him a sense of responsibility from a very young age and set him apart from his peers. Akshay takes pride in the fact that his parents have provided him and his sister with a strong and stable family background and admits in almost every interview that witnessing how his parents never let their disability stand in their way inspired in him the desire to become financially independent from a very young age. His father, Kaushik, is a care worker and his mother, Renuka, is a teaching assistant and also works with Camden Council, where she is a support worker for deaf children.

Akshay encountered the world of real estate and discovered what role he could play in it by happenstance! When he was about 10 or 11, the family bought their own house. Being the negotiator and spokesman for his family, Akshay discovered the huge commission that estate agents charged. He was appalled and decided at the time that the system could be improved.

Growing up in a world of technological advancements where disruptors like Uber and Amazon are thriving, Akshay thought of a way in which buyers and sellers of houses could be connected directly, without any middleman agent. At 16, the young would-be entrepreneur developed an app called HouseSmart that connected buyers and sellers directly. When all other kids his age were enjoying after their GCSEs, Akshay spent six weeks locked up with his cousin, building his app, though he decided to scrap it even before its launch. Akshay felt he needed to study and know the market better. After extensive research, learning floor plans and photography from scratch, in 2015, he ultimately created Doorsteps, the online portal.

Take every experience and turn it into an advantage.

Akshay had learnt the art of multitasking very early on in life. Being a young caregiver had imbibed in him a strong work ethic and time-management skills. In sixth grade, while most of his classmates played and had fun during the free periods, young Akshay could be found sitting and studying financial forecasting. Even when a due date for an essay was in two weeks, Akshay preferred finishing it in advance, at the risk of his classmates thinking that he was crazy. Now a successful businessman, he advises young people to do their hardest task in the morning because that way, he feels, the rest of the day gets much easier.

The other thing that Akshay was always good at was finding solutions to his problems. And the biggest proof of that is Doorsteps. But the creative-minded Akshay started his entrepreneurial journey much before 16. Once, when he was about 11 or 12, he demanded a PlayStation from his parents. When they refused to buy it for him, Akshay decided to earn and buy it for himself. Realizing that his most captive customers were the students in school, he decided to earn the money for his PlayStation by selling sweets to them and quickly earned enough to get himself the PlayStation.

Where there's a problem, there's always a solution.

Akshay advises young people to read a lot of books, especially biographies, which he finds most inspiring because they prove that successful people are actually regular people who have done extraordinary things by deciding to step out of their comfort zone and take a risk. The inspiration behind Doorsteps's USP—its low subscription price of £99—came to Akshay when he read the biography of RyanAir CEO Michael O'Leary while studying for his financial exams. Leary had become successful by offering and providing flights for just £4.99. It struck Akshay that if customers are offered a great product or service at an unbelievably low price, then it immediately grasps their interest. While property agents in the UK were charging a 2 to 3 per cent commission, which on an average London property equates to about £10,000, Doorsteps decided to charge only £99. With an aim to do away with the traditional way in which houses were being sold in England, Akshay decided to set up a basic website that would offer to sell properties only for a fraction of the cost charged by established agents. 'Why give an estate agent a small fortune just for putting photos of your house on the internet?' Akshay says in an interview with *Daily Mail Online*.[2]

---

[2] Chris Brooke, 'Teenager Who Set Up £12m Estate Agency... While Still in the Sixth Form! Entrepreneur Is Already Worth Millions after Selling Houses during His Lunch Break', *Daily Mail Online*, 15 October 2017. Available at https://www.dailymail.co.uk/news/article-4982920/Teenager-set-12m-estate-agency-sixth-form.html; accessed on 11 March 2021.

Find your unique selling point.

Akshay plunged into the world of real estate after borrowing £7,000 from his relatives for the set-up cost. Once the first sale was made, the business started to grow as a result of word-of-mouth advertising, and in almost a year, Doorsteps was ranked the eighteenth biggest estate agency in the UK. Initially, Akshay was just a one-man army, often knocking on people's doors himself, asking if they wanted to sell their house for £99 and mostly being responded to with the door slammed on his face. Despite being adept at multitasking, Akshay was still a student and had classes and exams to take care of. Ingeniously, he hired a call centre to answer calls while he was at school and he would return them when he was free. He also hired self-employed mothers to show prospective clients around the listed properties. He felt that mothers were more trustworthy and honest and would make the experience better for potential buyers, leading to more sales. In interviews, Akshay is not shy to admit, unlike many of his age, that mothers know much more than we will ever realize, and hence, when they give any advice, we should take it. His own mother is extremely proud of him. When she first heard of his idea, she thought it was something very different as he was helping others by saving them their money.

Since its launch in 2015, by charging only £99 for listing their properties, Akshay has indeed been able to save customers millions of pounds in fees. But, like any other business, success didn't come without challenges. Although Akshay did not consider age to be an impediment, others often viewed his business with disbelief simply because of his young age. Akshay was also worried whether his business model would work and be viable. The email from his first seller proved to him that his innovative, high-concept, online business model had, in fact, worked. People thought that being successful with a well-branded, clean online proposition at £99 in the UK market was impossible, yet Doorsteps managed to prove everyone wrong with their enormous and quick growth and success rate. Akshay's company has already sold over £1 billion worth of properties in different areas of the UK. Some of the most expensive houses he has sold are priced at more than a £1 million. Where a property takes an average of 57 days to sell, Doorsteps often manages to make a sale in 20 days. Within just a year of being established, the company, which is described in the media as 'the Uber of the property world', got valued at £12 million. After the company valuation, crowdfunding investors purchased almost £400,000 worth of shares, which Akshay used to scale up the business. Initially, Akshay paid himself a salary of only £500 a month, but when things started going well, he upped it to £1,000 a month.

Take risks. To make a million you must take risks.

Faced with difficult decisions to make when he was just 18 and worrying about whether his business would fail, about whether he should go to university instead, about whether he would be the oldest at his university, Akshay finally concluded that he wanted to live life on his own terms. His desire to succeed was initially driven by wanting to make his parents lives better but today he has also decided to share his learnings with others and empower disruption by setting up Ruparelia Coaching & Consulting. 'I damn well enjoy making a difference. So I'll keep driving ahead, and sit tight for the long term rewards. What makes it even more exhilarating?... the fact that it could all be gone tomorrow,' Akshay admits in a Facebook post on his own page. Today, to add to his skills, Akshay has decided to accept a place at Oxford University for the 10KSB business programme, which is fully funded by Goldman Sachs.

Although Akshay spends most of his time at work—almost 13 hours a day, seven days a week—he likes to recharge by playing tennis and hanging out with his friends. But he is also not one to while away too much time. He advises young people, 'Don't waste time watching shows like *Love Island* on TV, work hard, make money and maybe you'll be able to buy your own island and invite whoever you want to join you on it.'[3] For the breakthroughs he has made at such a young age, his friends teasingly call him Alan Sugar, after Lord Sugar, the business tycoon and star of the British TV series *The Apprentice*. They surely seem to have got it right, for, like Lord Sugar, Akshay too has made it to the *Sunday Times* Rich List as of May 2018, being the youngest person ever to do so.

Helen Keller once said, 'Character cannot be developed in ease and quiet. Only through experience of trial and suffering can the soul be strengthened, ambition inspired, and success achieved.' And what set Akshay apart from the average youngster are definitely the challenges that he has faced, which he admits has led to character building, something he values most dearly and which has made him one of the 100 most influential people of London at the young age of 22.

If you really care about something and you care about making a difference, you'll make it work.

---

[3]Jeremy Armstrong, 'Teen Tycoon Is Britain's 'Youngest Millionaire' after Selling Houses during His School Lunchbreaks', 15 October 2017. Available at https://www.mirror.co.uk/news/uk-news/teen-tycoon-britains-youngest-millionaire-11346804; accessed on 11 March 2021.

Chapter 2

THE POWER OF FAILURE

Bhavish Aggarwal: Founder of Ola

In 2007, two young students of Indian Institute of Technology (IIT) Bombay, Bhavish Aggarwal and Ankit Bhati, set out on a bicycle tour of 335 km from their campus in Powai to Ratnagiri in coastal Maharashtra. They had been meticulously and rigorously planning and training for the trip for weeks in advance. And, finally, around Diwali, they hit the road. On the first day, they crossed Alibaug, Kashid, along the north Konkan coast and Murud-Janjira in Raigad district, covering more than half the distance they had targeted. But a day later, their energy and enthusiasm fizzled out and they were on their way back, taking a bus home instead of riding their bicycles.

Even though Bhavish and Ankit abandoned their grand bicycle tour, there is one journey that has been hugely successful for them—their business venture Ola, a word that sounds like the word for 'hello' in Spanish. Ola was first started by Bhavish as olatrips.com, a portal that helped in reservation of cars and hotels for outstation trips. Once, after he had rented a car for a weekend trip to Bandipur from Bengaluru, the driver stopped midway in Mysore and demanded to be paid more. Unrelenting, Bhavish covered the rest of the distance by bus. This bitter experience seems to have been a sign from the universe for it inspired the entrepreneur in him to realize the need for a quality cab service. Ankit joined him, and the duo created Ola Cabs in 2011.

*The universe always gives us a sign.
Look out for the right signs.*

Bhavish had met Ankit on their first day at IIT. Their rooms were next to each other and Ankit had walked across and knocked on Bhavish's door to introduce himself. Best friends ever since, they shared a mentor and often teamed up at tech fests. Passionate and enterprising, the young students dreamt of starting their own company together. Hungry for real-world experience, they took part in a number of extracurricular works, including freelance coding projects. Bhavish recalls that they did not get paid for the first project they worked on, but what they gained instead was invaluable—experiences that taught them about the core principles of real business and a lifelong friendship to treasure.

Born to doctor parents, Naresh Kumar Aggarwal and Usha Aggarwal, on 28 August 1985, Bhavish spent his early years in Afghanistan and the UK and moved to Punjab in India in the third grade. His father was very strict. He recalls how ecstatic he was when he got admission into IIT Bombay to study Computer Science. His father, however, did not seem too elated with his rank. On hearing that Bhavish had ranked twenty-third, his father felt he could do better. Many years later, when he first told his parents about starting his new ride-sharing venture, his father commented, 'You finished IIT just to start a travel agency?'[1] His worried parents, strangers to

---

[1] Durba Ghosh, 'Even Bhavish Aggarwal's Father Wants to Know When Ola Will Turn Profitable', *Quartz India*, 23 January 2019. Available at https://qz.com/india/1530371/bhavish-aggarwal-opens-up-about-olas-journey-to-om-swami/; accessed on 11 March 2021.

the new technological developments happening in the modern world, couldn't comprehend why their son would leave the lucrative job he had at Microsoft Research—which he had bagged soon after graduating from IIT in 2008—and start his own business. So upset were they that they refused to speak to him for six months. After Bhavish became successful and Ola finally reached his hometown, his parents got to know about it through their driver, who quit the job to buy his own car and register as a driver with Ola. That's when his mother gradually came around to downloading her son's app and learned to summon a car whenever she wanted one. This sense of new-found liberation that his mother has experienced makes Bhavish very proud.

Resistance does not last forever.

Despite the initial opposition from home and the challenges he faced, Bhavish was adamant to make his venture work. In the initial days, Bhavish could be found pitching his idea and showing the early version of the Ola app to anyone and everyone who showed any interest. He was determined to succeed. Such was his dedication towards his customers that, in the early days, he would often borrow his then girlfriend Rajalakshmi's car to fulfil trip requests and fill in when drivers were unavailable.

Today, Rajalakshmi and Bhavish are married. She has seen him through his days of struggle and has been a witness to Ola's journey from the beginning. On dates, before marriage, Bhavish would often admit to being broke and let Rajalakshmi pay for the coffee. He thought of it as an investment for the future, he says in jest in an interview with *Bloomberg TV*.[2] It

---

[2] https://www.youtube.com/watch?v=32-r9UlqrsQ; accessed on 11 March 2021.

took Bhavish ten movie dates to finally gather the courage to tell Rajalakshmi how he felt.

After their marriage, Rajalakshmi wanted to buy a Vespa, but Bhavish kept discouraging her. He wanted her to use the Ola services instead. It took three years for him to convince her about the benefits of Ola, but he finally did it. He still doesn't own a car but instead uses the Ola services to understand the challenges that his customers face so he can improve the product better.

Practise what you preach.

Bhavish began Ola with an initial investment of about ₹2 to 3 lakh from his savings. The company had only about 20 employees in the first three to four years and the early days were filled with various problems. Figuring out where next month's salaries would come from was what was primarily on Bhavish's mind. Bhavish and Ankit were clear about the model on which they based Ola. Unlike other cab services, which had their own inventory of cars, Ola's USP was that they rented cars and partnered with a number of taxi drivers. Consumers could book cars at a short notice via their call centres or their app, but in the initial days, even before launching the app, they offered rides on demand to customers who called them on the phone.

Ola's humble beginnings and its initial hiccups are what probably kept them grounded and helped them focus on the essentials: consumers and a good financial system. Ola was founded on ingenious ideas and a fighting spirit. Bhavish used a unique strategy to woo drivers. For the first few months, the drivers would not get any salary but be paid ₹5,000 per day in the form of tips if they met the criteria of completing one single trip for that given day. Due to the potential monthly income that they could make, many drivers wanted to be associated with Ola. The payment module was later reduced to half and a salary was added consecutively. Bhavish very intelligently also took in those cars which had an all-India permit for both travel within and outside the city.

Bhavish's overzealous and never-give-up attitude is what kept the company moving towards newer directions. With his foresight, he could clearly see the value that m-commerce would add to the company. And as predicted, Ola saw its first spurt in growth between 2014 and 2017, when connectivity and access to information became easier with the mobile revolution becoming a huge deal in India. Bhavish and Ankit made their app efficient enough to work on 2G networks for use in small towns and also designed the company in a way that it could fulfil the urgent needs of big cities. Gradually, with the demand for increased transportation, the company went from a few hundred vehicles to a million drivers.

Be intuitive to the needs of the customers.

Today, Ola boasts of over 10 to 15 million customers every month and the focus is more on sustainability and long-term performance with an aim to outlive their competitors. Clarity of thought and a strong vision for the future makes the founders of Ola stand out from others. They seem to follow a simple mantra: think like a customer, be like a customer.

Initially, fundraising was extremely tough for the business newbies. When an angel investor had once asked Bhavish to send across an 'org structure', so new was he to the world of business that he had to google the term to understand what it meant.

The company found loyal cheerleaders in their initial angel investors, Snapdeal founder Kunal Bahl, Rehan Yar

Khan and Anupam Mittal, and were able to raise ₹34 lakh. In 2015, after receiving a $5 million investment from Tiger Global Management, Bhavish knew that they had cracked the market and were doing something right. In an interview with *YourStory*, Bhavish said, 'For every round we raised, we never took money from the person (firm) offering us the highest valuation. We have always taken money from the person who believes in our journey and end vision, for the long haul.'[3] But despite the strong investments in the company, Bhavish doesn't want to sell to anybody. With every new funding round, Bhavish has brought in new investors to Ola, thereby curbing the influence and power of any single investor.

Set well-defined goals and have a clear vision.

Bhavish was clear from the beginning that Ola was not going to be only about cabs but about mobility. He said in an interview with *Fortune India*, 'We are still a startup, we need to do many more things.'[4] And they did. First came Ola Café, a food delivery service. Ola Café partnered with over 100 restaurants and offered a curated menu with the most popular dishes from the restaurants. The menu options keep changing every 20 minutes between noon and 10.30 p.m. Then came Ola Store, an on-demand grocery delivery app with handpicked products in partnership with local stores and trusted retailers. The next

---

[3]Sindhu Kashyaap and Tenzin Pema, 'TechSparks 2019: Bhavish Aggarwal Says "Absolutely Focused" on Taking Ola Public in the Next Two Years', *YourStory*, 12 October 2019. Available at https://yourstory.com/2019/10/techsparks-2019-bhavish-aggarwal-ola-ipo-going-public; accessed on 11 March 2021.

[4]Kunal N. Talgeri, Tanmoy Goswami and Rajiv Bhuva, 'Ola: Bhavish Aggarwal Learns to Fly', *Fortune India*, 5 August 2015. Available at https://www.fortuneindia.com/people/ola-bhavish-aggarwal-learns-to-fly/100389; accessed on 11 March 2021.

step for the experimental company was Ola Money, a mobile wallet that accounts for bill payments for 40 per cent of all Ola rides. Bhavish's dream was to create an institution, not merely build a business.

From their humble one-BHK office in Mumbai, Ola has now moved beyond India to Australia, the UK and New Zealand. The youthful, vibrant and ever-growing brand matches the personality of its founder. Bhavish is ever smiling and always energetic. Inspired by one of the greatest entrepreneurs, Steve Jobs—incidentally, *The Biography of Steve Jobs* is his favourite book—Bhavish burns with an ambition that makes him start his day at 7 a.m. and often continues late at night till 1 a.m. The passion that keeps him going is the aim to solve the big problems of the world. With that purpose in mind, Ola has now started Ola Foundation, the social welfare arm—led by Rajalakshmi—that aims to empower 500,000 women by 2025 by giving them access to sustainable livelihoods. The foundation has now set up a 'Drive the Driver' fund towards the welfare and upliftment of drivers and their families who have been affected by the restrictions of the pandemic. Bhavish has also foregone a year's salary to ensure that the amount can be deployed against combating the challenges that the pandemic has brought upon the company and the employees. Despite 2020 being an extremely tough year for Ola—the company having to cut about a third of its workforce—the 34-year-old Bhavish is still optimistic about Ola's long-term future. Not one to be defeated, he plans to work towards building a more sustainable future and become the leader in electric mobility in India by foraying into electric scooter manufacturing.

Aim to solve the big problems.

The very first time that Bhavish had appeared for the Joint Entrance Exams in order to gain admission into India's most prestigious network of technology colleges, the IITs, he had failed. The next year he returned better prepared and secured an all-India rank of 23. This truly sums up the perseverance that he embodies. Learning and moving on from his failures, he believes in failing fast but moving ahead fast. His best friend and co-founder, Ankit, describes him perfectly in the interview with *Fortune India*, 'He is always dreaming of where next Ola can be, and how fast we can get there. He is impatient at all the right times.'[5] Although the two friends abandoned their cycle journey in their early days as students, the Ola journey that they have embarked upon is not one they are willing to give up.

Fail fast and move ahead fast.

---

[5]Kunal N. Talgeri, Tanmoy Goswami and Rajiv Bhuva, 'Ola: Bhavish Aggarwal Learns to Fly', *Fortune India*, 5 August 2015. Available at https://www.fortuneindia.com/people/ola-bhavish-aggarwal-learns-to-fly/100389; accessed on 11 March 2021.

Chapter 3

SETTING THE RULES

Bill Gates: Co-founder of Microsoft and Gates Foundation

Once, at Harvard, a young boy who had enrolled to study law to become a lawyer like his father confidently told his teachers that he would become a millionaire by the time he turned 30. After two years, he dropped out of Harvard to co-found the software company Microsoft. The boy was Bill Gates and by 31, he was already a billionaire.

What motivated Bill to start Microsoft, however, was not the dream of becoming rich. In an interview in 1992, he said, 'There are a lot of people, when they talked about me said I'm an entrepreneur, as though I had this general desire to go out and start a business and make money and that wasn't the case at all. I had a fascination with computers and software.'[1]

His interest in computers and software was first solidified at Seattle's preparatory Lakeside School. At 13, the extremely shy and introverted Bill was unsure if he would be able to find the new school that he had moved to fun. But when he met his classmate Kent Evans and his senior Paul Allen, the trajectory of his life changed. In school, Bill spent a lot of time at the

---

[1] https://www.youtube.com/watch?v=9ckGnSY7heg; accessed on 11 March 2021.

newly installed computer terminal, at one time even being banned from using the computer because, along with some other students, he had hacked into it to get extra computing time. In return for more computer time, the students decided to look for bugs in the computer system. Bill's first ever programme was Tic-Tac-Toe in BASIC computer language, where users played against the computer.

Kent and Bill spent a lot of time thinking about what they could become when they grow up, reading magazines about technology and bonding over their love for computers. The two first hit it off when they were both recruited by Paul Allen, two years their senior, for the Lakeside Programmers Group. For their talent, Bill and Kent were tasked by the administrators of the school to create class schedules for over 400 students after Lakeside merged with the local all-girls school. While in the middle of working on their first big project together, Bill lost his best friend, Kent, to an unfortunate mountain-climbing accident. The loss left a big hole in his life; the best friends had 'big plans, big dreams' together, as Bill recalls in the Netflix documentary *Inside Bill's Brain: Decoding Bill Gates.* Yet, he didn't let the tragedy deter him from achieving great things. He adds, 'I sorta thought, hey OK, now I'm going to do these things that Kent and I talked about, but I'll do it without Kent.'[2] After Kent's passing, Bill reached out to Paul Allen, who was studying at Washington State University at the time, to come and help him. This began a lifelong partnership and friendship. And on 4 April 1975 in Albuquerque, New Mexico, the duo founded Microsoft.

Don't give up on your dreams, no matter what.

---

[2]*Inside Bill's Brain: Decoding Bill Gates,* dir. David Guggenheim (2019, Netflix).

Bill and Paul were intrinsically very different from each other. Paul was reserved and Bill was feisty, but what cemented their lifelong friendship was their love for computer programming. The first business venture that the two started together was Traf-o-Data, a computer programme that examined traffic patterns in Seattle. They earned $20,000 with it. When Allen showed Gates the 1 January 1975 issue of *Popular Electronics* that featured an article on the Altair 8800, the mini-computer kit created by Micro Instrumentation and Telemetry Systems (MITS), both friends wondered about the ripples this computer could create in the area of personal computing. Jumping at the chance, Paul and Bill—who had by then dropped out of Harvard—called up MITS and offered to create a software for the Altair 8800 that would run on BASIC. At the time, the enthusiastic and young risk-takers neither had an Altair to work on nor the code to run on it. When the company asked for a demonstration, they worked day and night and developed a prototype within eight weeks. Paul travelled to New Mexico for a test run. Luckily, and to everyone's surprise, it worked perfectly.

Many years later, when invited back to give a speech at the Lakeside School in 2005, Gates said, 'The experience and insight Paul Allen and I gained here gave us the confidence to start a company based on this wild idea that nobody else agreed with—that computer chips were going to become so powerful that computers and software would become a tool that would be on every desk and in every home.'[3]

Be confident about your ideas.

---

[3] https://www.gatesfoundation.org/media-center/speeches/2005/09/bill-gates-lakeside-school; accessed on 11 March 2021.

Microsoft first started with only 11 employees. Gates joked about their first office photograph that the average geek of the 1970s was definitely not on the front-line of fashion. Initially hyphenated, Micro-soft—a blend of 'micro-computer' and 'software'—was making approximately $2.5 million by 1979 and, at just 23, Gates was the head of the company. The beginnings of Microsoft, which had been moved to Seattle, were not smooth sailing, though. The company's BASIC software programme wasn't meeting the company overheads and piracy of the pre-market copies was rampant.

The first major breakthrough came for Microsoft when IBM approached them for software that could make various programmes run on their first PC. On 6 November 1980, Microsoft signed the contract and IBM agreed to pay them $430,000 for what would later come to be known as MS-DOS. Ingeniously, Microsoft held the exclusive licensing rights and also retained the rights to license the operating system to other computer manufacturers besides IBM. With more computers coming into the market, Microsoft's business grew. By 1983, 30 per cent of the world's computers were running on Microsoft, which went global with offices in different parts of the world.[4] In two years, trying to stay ahead of the competition, Microsoft announced the launch of a new operating system called Windows in response to the growing interest in graphical user interface and in direct competition with Apple that had, in just one year of its existence, done an extensive amount of work in the area with their Macintosh computers.

Known for his intelligence and his obsessively hardworking nature, Gates was able to visualize and understand all sides

---

[4] https://www.biography.com/business-figure/bill-gates; 11 March 2021.

of the software industry, including product development and corporate strategy. One day, early on in Microsoft's life, Bill's assistant found someone sleeping under a desk. When she was just about to call security, she realized it was Bill himself. Bill also became notorious for keeping a track of employees' license plates to see who was spending how much time at work. He pushed and challenged people to work like he did and keep the creative process going. Many years later he admitted, 'Eventually I had to loosen up, as the company got to a reasonable size.'[5] When asked about his workaholic past, Bill admitted in an 'Ask Me Anything' on Reddit, 'Now hopefully I am a bit more mellow but with a little extra wisdom.'[6]

Work hard. Work harder than everyone else.
Work the hardest.

Born to Mary Maxwell and William H. Gates Sr on 28 October 1955 in Seattle, Washington, Bill's strong-headedness and competitive nature landed him in a lot of trouble as a child. An introvert who spent most of his time cooped up in his room reading books or just thinking, Bill was a difficult child to handle and was often at loggerheads with his mother. He recalls that in Christmas cards that were sent out with family news every year, the update usually was: his father's law firm is growing, his mother's volunteer work is going strong, the girls are doing well in school but Bill is a handful. One night, when he was in the sixth grade, his mother asked exasperatedly, 'What are you doing?' after trying to get him to come out and eat dinner with the family. 'I'm thinking,' Bill answered.

---
[5] https://www.bbc.co.uk/programmes/b06z1zdt; accessed on 11 March 2021.
[6] Mark Hachman, 'Bill Gates: OS, Data to Wander between Devices', *PC World*, 10 February 2014. Available at https://www.pcworld.com/article/2095492/bill-gates-os-data-to-wander-between-devices.html; accessed on 11 March 2021.

'You're thinking?' 'Yes, Mom, I'm thinking,' he said aggressively and insolently quipped, 'Have you tried thinking?' When his family sought counselling for his irreverent and problematic behaviour, the psychologist eventually concluded that here was an extremely intelligent boy, very different from others, and told his parents, 'You're going to lose. You had better adjust to it because there's no use trying to punish him. It's useless to try to compete with him.'[7]

Despite Bill's difficult relationship with his mother in his childhood, she was the one who had the greatest impact on him throughout his life. Bill's mother Mary, who was a teacher for a brief period in her life, devoted the rest of her life to raising her three children, Bill and his two sisters, Kristianne and Libby, while also working on civic affairs and with charities. Serving as a board member for several corporates, including the First Interstate Bank in Seattle, the United Way and IBM, she was an outgoing and magnetic personality who often encouraged Bill to be social and meet with people. Incidentally, she was the one who introduced him to the CEO of IBM! Once, when she asked him to meet Warren Buffett, the world's most successful stock trader, Bill told her he was too busy. Eventually, he did meet him and now the two are best of friends bonding over philanthropy, technology and playing Bridge in their free time.

Mothers know best.

Mary would often take Bill along with her when she volunteered at schools and community organizations and worked for charities. She instilled in him the need to work for others, which has made him a philanthropic powerhouse

---

[7]*Inside Bill's Brain: Decoding Bill Gates*, dir. David Guggenheim (2019, Netflix).

today. In 2000, along with his wife[8] and partner, Melinda Gates, Bill founded the Gates Foundation, the world's largest private charitable enterprise. Although the foundation had worked towards scholarships for young students and helped install 47,000 computers in 11,000 libraries across 50 states in the US, both Bill and Melinda didn't feel like they were really creating an impact. It was after leaving his full-time job at Microsoft in 2008 that Bill was able to focus on more serious issues plaguing the world. Today, Gates Foundation has made major progress in tackling issues of poverty, polio eradication, clean water, hygiene, health, women's empowerment, climate change, among many others all over the world. According to the website Gates Notes, Bill finds his work at Microsoft quite similar to his work at the foundation. 'In both cases, he gets to bring together smart people and collaborate with them to solve big, tough problems.'[9] Bill calls it 'optimization' and admits it is what motivates him to keep working.

In 2010, Bill and Melinda also teamed up with Warren Buffett to start 'The Giving Pledge' campaign, encouraging the wealthiest of the world to donate at least half of their wealth to pressing issues of philanthropy. As of August 2020, the pledge has 211 signatories from across 23 countries. Bill Gates has also become one of the leading forces in the fight against the coronavirus pandemic. Ever since COVID-19 hit, both Bill and Melinda Gates have lent their expertise and resources and spoken with health leaders around the world to help fight the pandemic. The Gates Foundation has invested billions in its efforts to help in the global efforts to enable rapid testing

---

[8] On 3 May 2021, Bill and Melinda posted a statement on Twitter announcing the end of their marriage.

[9] https://www.gatesnotes.com/Bio; accessed on 11 March 2021.

and develop and distribute safe, affordable and timely vaccines for most countries. Guided by the belief that every life has equal value, the Bill & Melinda Gates Foundation is working tirelessly to help all people lead healthy, productive lives.

In his Netflix documentary, when asked what is the one thing he would like to do before he dies, Gates says succinctly, 'Thank Melinda'. An equal partner in life and in work, Bill first met Melinda French when she sat next to him at an Expo trade-fair dinner. Melinda, who worked as a product marketing manager at Microsoft at the time, found Bill to be funnier than she had expected. Months later, the two ran into each again when they parked close to each other at the Microsoft parking lot. After a long conversation, Bill asked Melinda if she would go out on a date with him after two weeks. Melinda rebuffed his request for not being spontaneous enough. When she reached home an hour later, he called her apartment and said, 'Is this spontaneous enough for you?'[10]

Melinda recalls that despite how he may seem to outsiders, he immediately let his guard down with her on the first date. In 1994, the couple got married in Hawaii after Bill had convinced himself that it was the best thing to do. His whiteboard, with his pros and cons list that he made in order to decide whether to get married, said so! It indeed turned out to be the best decision of his life as Bill is not hesitant to admit after 25 years of marriage and three children together. Through all their ups and downs, what helped them power through, Melinda says, is keeping 'a united front', both at work and at home.

An especially hard time for the couple was when Microsoft faced a string of Federal Trade Commission and Justice Department investigations for allegedly making unfair

---

[10]*Inside Bill's Brain: Decoding Bill Gates*, dir. David Guggenheim (2019, Netflix).

deals with computer manufacturers and illegally maintaining a monopoly in the market. The company was even ordered to be split into two—one to produce the operating system and the other to produce other software components. The decision was later overturned on appeal and Gates admits that he broke down and cried when the company was finally vindicated.

Every year, Bill takes a couple of 'Think Weeks' where he retreats to a cabin in a forest in the Pacific Northwest with his books and papers to think about innovative ideas and solutions. The Think Week is his CPU time, he says. In fact, work done during the Think Week is what eventually led Microsoft to launch the Internet Explorer. Melinda says that his mind is a chaotic place, there is too much happening at once there. Coupled with a unique complex mind is Bill's passion for work. In an interview with *Vanity Fair*, Paul Allen wrote of a telling exchange that Bill had with a colleague, Bob Greenberg. After Bob had put in 81 hours of work in four days, Bill touched base with him and asked what he was going to work on the next day. Bob said that he was planning to take the day off, to which Bill genuinely and naively asked, 'Why would you want to do that?' Allen writes, Bill 'never really seemed to need to recharge.'[11] Even to this day and after so many achievements, when faced with challenges, he has a simple solution: work harder. Armed with this solution, Bill Gates is tackling one major world problem after another and solving them not only for himself but for humanity.

*When faced with challenges,
put in more effort and more work.*

---

[11]Paul Allen, 'Microsoft's Odd Couple', *Vanity Fair*, 30 March 2011. Available at https://www.vanityfair.com/news/2011/05/paul-allen-201105; accessed on 11 March 2021.

Chapter 4

WORK IS PLAY, PLAY IS WORK

Blake Ross: Co-founder of Firefox

At 35, Blake Ross has already worked for some of the giants of the tech world and the biggest names in Silicon Valley—Netscape, Facebook and Uber. In fact, he pretty much came of age in Silicon Valley, having moved there when he was just 14. By then, Ross, logging on to his family's *America Online* (AOL) account, was already fixing bugs on Netscape's browsers. Netscape had ruled the browser industry from 1995 to 1997 but when Microsoft made its browser Internet Explorer free, Netscape lost out. After being bought over by AOL, Netscape decided to release its browsers as 'open source' so that volunteer developers from across the country could hack into it and try their hand at fixing it. The community of next-gen developers who would help build Netscape's future browsers were called the Mozilla group. Young Blake Ross was one of them. Blake talked about the incredible life-changing experience with *Wired*, 'It's a great feeling to make a little change to the code and then actually see the change in the window of a big, famous product. You've caused something to happen in an application that's being used all over the world.'[1]

---

[1] Josh McHugh, 'The Firefox Explosion', *Wired*, 1 February 2005. Available at https://www.wired.com/2005/02/firefox/; accessed on 11 March 2021.

By the end of his high school years at Gulliver Preparatory School in Miami, Florida, Blake had already landed himself a summer internship at Netscape. When he told his father that he had landed a job at 14, his father recalls thinking if it was at the local store or someplace like that, never expecting that his son's hobby of fixing bugs would actually land him a job at Netscape. When the teenage Blake moved to California, his mother moved across the country with him, rented an apartment near her son's workplace and drove him to work daily.

Cultivate hobbies. Indulge in them.

At Netscape, Blake realized that the unfriendliness of the browser was pushing users away. The browser was full of ads and unnecessary search buttons. He came up with the idea to add a pop-up blocker, but the idea did not go down well with those in charge. The frustration of not being able to deliver on a user-friendly browser led Blake to team up with friends and fellow programmers Dave Hyatt and Joe Hewitt to start recreating the Mozilla browser as a side project. They built a standalone, minimalist, simple browser with a straightforward interface. The new browser was launched in 2002 and was called Phoenix, a reference to the mythical firebird that rises from its ashes—in this case, the metaphorical ashes of Netscape. But the trademark was already owned by someone else. So, next they came up with the name Firebird. This name too was taken. More months of brainstorming led them to come up with Firefox—the nickname of the red panda that also became its mascot. Firefox was officially released on 9 November 2004.

Any idea can become big if we never give up on it.

In less than a year, Firefox hit 100 million downloads. Blake came up with the idea of hiring people to try and hack into their browser to discover bugs. Ross, along with a fellow founder, Asa Dotzler, also started a page called 'Spread Firefox' to tap into the talents of those who were not coders. Over 250,000 people signed up. In the weeks following the debut, Firefox contributors and fans threw their own launch parties in 392 cities around the world. Over 10 days in October, more than 10,000 donors put in enough money to pay for a two-page spread in the *New York Times*. Firefox became famous through word of mouth and was marketed by the users themselves. When Firefox 2.0 appeared, it clocked two million downloads in the first 24 hours. Web surfers were switching to Firefox at the rate of seven million a month. In the book *Founders at Work: Stories of Startups' Early Days*, Ross admitted to author Jessica Livingstone that he always thought marketing was something very difficult, but if the product is good enough, people usually spread it on their own.[2]

A good product will advertise itself,
so concentrate on making a good product.

Born to a lawyer father, David, and a psychologist mother, Abby, on 12 June 1985 in Miami, Ross is the youngest of three children. He developed an interest in computers as early as four years old. By the time he was 10, he had already developed his first website via AOL. He then went on to create simple, text-based games to play in AOL chat rooms. Blake admits in a *STANFORD Magazine* interview in 2005, 'I was never really content to just *use* the computer. I was always

---

[2]Jessica Livingston, *Founders at Work: Stories of Startups' Early Days* (2001, Apress).

tinkering with it in some way.'[3]

As a young child, oblivious to his parents, Blake would often sit in his room till late into the night and teach himself to code in HTML and Microsoft Visual Basic. His mother recalls how everyone told her that he would become the next Bill Gates. 'I don't like telling people what I'm doing until I have something to show them,' Ross said in an interview in 2006.[4] His parents finally read about his role in creating Firefox in a magazine!

Although a computer geek himself, Blake understood early enough how computer browsers made by computer geeks were not what everyday people wanted. The greatest example of this was his mother. Despite being extremely educated, she was often stumped when trying to do anything online. She would frequently call out to him from across the hallway when she couldn't find her Internet Explorer bookmarks, when she was getting besieged with pop-up ads or when her computer was being attacked by viruses. Ross was the go-to guy for tech support both in his house and with friends. His express purpose behind creating the new browser was to make people's lives easy, especially those of his parents. With Firefox, Ross and his team had been able to create a browser that could be used both by inexperienced users and which could also be modified to satisfy more advanced users. The Firefox source code was available for all to download and so people from all over the world could create extensions that worked with the browser.

---

[3]Greta Lorge, 'Mister Firefox', *STANDFORD Magazine*, May/June 2005. Available at https://stanfordmag.org/contents/mister-firefox; accessed on 11 March 2021.
[4]https://spectrum.ieee.org/computing/software/the-firefox-kid; accessed on 11 March 2021.

Having a purpose makes setting goals easier.

Ross published a book called *Firefox for Dummies* in 2006. In his book, he mentions that the goal they had written down while creating Firefox was to 'have fun and build an excellent, user-friendly browser without all the constraints (features, compatibility, marketing, month-long discussions, etc.) that afflict the current browser development.'[5] He also admits that good ideas start with the customer. And for Ross, the greatest idea came from his desire to make the Internet easier to use for his parents.

The customers are the source of every good idea.

While on campus at Stanford, where Ross enrolled as a Computer Science major in 2003, he admits he would often fight the urge to look over people's shoulders when they were browsing the Internet just to see what browser they were using. Later, he stopped out of university to pair up with fellow Firefox contributor Joe Hewitt and created Parakey, a user interface designed to bridge the gap between the computer and the Internet, so that transferring pictures, videos and written material to the web would become easier.

Blake's enterprising nature was evident from very early on. On his Facebook page, he shared a picture of himself from the early '90s surrounded by Archie Comics books. As a kid, he started an Archie Comics newsletter and printed and mailed it to subscribers he found on the Internet. His first subscriber was a Noam Gumpel from Tel Aviv who paid the young Ross $2 per month for a six-month subscription. Ross's sincere endeavours caught the eye of the massive Archie

---

[5] Blake Ross, *Firefox for Dummies* (2006, Wiley Publishing, Inc.), p. 8

Comics powerhouse based in New York, which invited him out on a tour and sent him away with a sizeable heap of memorabilia and a subscription to their own newsletter that promised exclusive sneak peeks at upcoming story lines.

By age 21, Ross had already been nominated for *Wired* magazine's top Rave Award, Renegade of the Year, opposite Larry Page, Sergey Brin and Jon Stewart. At the time, he was balancing the responsibility of his huge start-up, understanding the ropes of the start-up world, meeting investors and trying desperately to manage his time so that he could make time for his parents and girlfriend.

In July 2007, Facebook bought Parakey, its first ever acquisition. Blake was initially hired to oversee development of the new user experience at Facebook but soon became its director of product. In one of his Facebook posts in 2011, he writes in his typical sharp, witty style:

'Hey subscribers: tell me about you.

About me: I'm a director of product at Facebook; I've worked here for 4 years on many things, like the new smart lists that we just launched. Ask about anything & I'll do my best to answer or route to a person who can. Prior to FB, I was a founder of Firefox, I didn't learn to ride a bike until I was 10 and my cat died of kidney failure. This answers the common questions, but let me know if I missed anything. I also love playing the piano and non-sequiturs.'[6]

In 2016, he added a little more about himself in a Facebook note titled, 'Aphantasia: How It Feels to Be Blind in Your Mind'.[7] Blake writes in the note about how he experiences

---
[6]Blake Ross (@blake), 'Hey Subscribers: Tell Me about You', *Facebook*, 17 September 2011. Available at https://www.facebook.com/blake; accessed on 11 March 2021.
[7]Blake Ross (@blake), 'Aphantasia: How It Feels to Be Blind in Your Mind', *Facebook*, 23 April 2016. Available at https://www.facebook.com/notes/blake-

Aphantasia, or the absence of fantasy, the inability to imagine. He writes how, unlike most people, he is unable to visualize and why he has always been better at concepts and facts than images. He recalls how, on a childhood IQ test, his best performance was on memory-driven aspects of the test like coding and digit span and his worst were on ones that required imagination and visualizing like picture completion, picture arrangement and object assembly.

His different way of perceiving the world gives him a unique identity and an advantage. Interested in writing fiction and film editing and production, just for fun, and of course entertainment, Ross wrote his own fanfiction episode of HBO's *Silicon Valley*, giving a hilarious insight into the real-life antics of the people at Silicon Valley.

After leaving Facebook in 2013 to 'try new things'[8] according to his goodbye letter that he posted on his own Facebook page, in 2017, he joined Uber to work on product strategy after being an outspoken observer of Uber on social media for a long time. The rest of the time, he works on his non-tech interests. When asked about Firefox, Blake says in the book by Jessica Livingston, 'We weren't trying to strike it rich with Firefox. It's open source and it's free. We weren't trying to take over the world; we had kind of modest goals, and it was OK if it failed. We were a lot freer to make risky decisions. If you can afford to do things that way, it's just so much better. You're not thinking about venture capitalists or

---

ross/aphantasia-how-it-feels-to-be-blind-in-your-mind/10156834777480504/; accessed on 11 March 2021.

[8]Kevin Smith, 'Facebook's Product Director Is Leaving and He Wrote a Really Funny Goodbye Note', *Business Insider*, 23 February 2013. Available at https://www.businessinsider.com/blake-ross-leaving-facebook-2013-2; accessed on 11 March 2021.

marketing or sales. Just product and users, all day every day."[9]

It is this way of approaching the world, of looking for a solution where a problem can be seen and of thinking about the user, the audience, at the end of the day that made Blake such a hit in the world of innovation.

Look for a solution where you can see a problem.

Quietly, in his own way, he is perhaps working on his next big project. And the world will know about it when he shows it to us. After all, as he admitted at just age 21, he had already been in the software industry for a generation—for 12 years—and didn't want to spend his entire life in the industry, simply because he thinks life is too short to do anything for too long.

Life is too short. Try new things.

---

[9] Jessica Livingston, *Founders at Work: Stories of Startups' Early Days* (2008, Apress), p. 400.

Chapter 5

DESIGNING DREAMS

Brian Chesky: Co-founder of Airbnb

In his high school yearbook, right under a picture of Brian Chesky smiling is a quote attributed to Jerry Seinfeld, 'I'm sure I'll amount to nothing.' Although Chesky wrote it in an attempt to be funny, it didn't go down well with his father, who was very upset and asked him exasperatedly, 'Nothing?! Nothing?!'[1]

Brian didn't amount to nothing! He went on to co-found Airbnb and appeared on *TIME*'s list of 100 most influential people for 2015 and on *Forbes*'s list of America's richest entrepreneurs under 40.

Yet Chesky is no textbook entrepreneur. Born on 29 August 1981 in Niskayuna, New York, to professional social workers, Robber H. Chesky and Deborah Chesky, Brian is the older of two siblings, with a younger sister Allison. His first passion since childhood was hockey. So obsessed was he that for Christmas one year, after receiving a full set of gear—pads, skates, stick and helmet—he insisted on sleeping in it. He also

---

[1]*The Economic Times*, 'Brian Chesky Can't Keep Cool because He'll Be Speaking at His Alma Mater', 5 June 2017. Available at https://economictimes.indiatimes.com/magazines/panache/brian-chesky-cant-keep-cool-because-hell-be-speaking-at-his-alma-mater/articleshow/58995509.cms?from=mdr; accessed on 15 March 2021.

had a vision for art and design and applied it to anything he could lay his hands on. Always wanting to fix things that didn't seem right to him, he would break open game gears and Game Boys and even redesign and draw on his Nike sneakers. He would spend hours at the local museum drawing replicas of the paintings. Drawing and designing were not just a passing phase for him as his mother put it aptly in an interview with *Fortune*, 'From a very young age, you could see that he didn't just dabble in something.'[2]

Follow your passion with dedication.

His love and aptitude for design was encouraged by his teachers at the local Niskayuna High School. Brian shared on his Facebook page a post about one art teacher who was the perfect mentor to him and believed that he could be a real artist someday. She convinced him to take up design and, on graduating from school, he enrolled into the Rhode Island School of Design (RISD) for a BFA degree with an emphasis on Industrial Design. His decision of going to art school was met with some scepticism, with his father telling him, 'I'll support you in going to RISD, but make sure one day you get a job with health insurance.'[3]

Chesky was no ordinary art school student. He pursued bodybuilding. He also helped develop the college's hockey team while his friend Jeo Gebbia ran the basketball team. Little did the two know then that they would one day go

---

[2] Leigh Gallagher, 'The Education of Airbnb's Brian Chesky', *Fortune*, 26 June 2015. Available at https://fortune.com/longform/brian-chesky-airbnb/; accessed on 15 March 2021.
[3] Sarah Lacy, 'An Unbelievable Journey: Interview with Brian Chesky', *Startups*, 2 January 2017. Available at https://www.startups.com/library/founder-stories/brian-chesky; accessed on 15 March 2021.

on to set up one of the largest companies in the world. The budding entrepreneurs in them had emerged, though, with the setting up of the athletic teams. Gebbia said later in an interview with *Fast Company*, 'These were basically our first startups.'[4] Aside from setting up teams, raising funding and putting schedules together, their main challenge was getting arts students to a game on Friday night—and they did it by rebranding the team, bringing in a new mascot and serving free beer! It was their first big marketing challenge and they succeeded.

When Brian enrolled into RISD, his father had said to him, 'It's a good thing you went to art school because usually the smart kid speaks at graduation.'[5] He was chosen as that commencement speaker, a task he threw himself into, studying every commencement speech he could find to make the experience less intimidating. The night before, he stood at the podium and watched as the staff set up 6,000 chairs one by one. The commencement speech turned out to be quite a success as Chesky walked onto the stage to Michael Jackson's 'Billie Jean' being played in the background and burst out into some moves, winning an instant cheer from his classmates. In his dramatic speech riddled with jokes, he admitted that the most important lesson he had learnt at college was that 'creativity will always work you to a solution.'[6]

---

[4]Austin Carr, 'Watch Airbnb CEO Brian Chesky Salute RISD, Whip off His Robe, Dance Like Michael Jackson', *Fast Company*, 17 February 2012. Available at https://www.fastcompany.com/1816858/watch-airbnb-ceo-brian-chesky-salute-risd-whip-his-robe-dance-michael-jackson; accessed on 15 March 2021.

[5]Austin Carr, 'Watch Airbnb CEO Brian Chesky Salute RISD, Whip off His Robe, Dance Like Michael Jackson', *Fast Company*, 17 February 2012. Available at https://www.fastcompany.com/1816858/watch-airbnb-ceo-brian-chesky-salute-risd-whip-his-robe-dance-michael-jackson; accessed on 15 March 2021.

[6]https://www.youtube.com/watch?v=BVxVR3UmIHI; accessed on 15 March 2021.

Truly, had it not been for this creativity, Airbnb would not come to exist!

Creativity will always help you find a solution.

Three years after graduating and parting ways, Joe called Brian to San Francisco. Chesky, at the time, had fulfilled his father's wish of getting a job with health insurance. He was working for 3DID in Los Angeles as an industrial designer and earning about $40,000 a year. One day, while driving, he had a moment of epiphany as he saw the road in front of him disappear into the horizon, only to see the same road from the rear-view mirror winding behind him. He thought his life had become exactly like the road—monotonous and tedious. So, he gladly threw in the towel, packed his belongings in an old Honda Civic and moved to San Francisco with only $1,000 in his bank.

In October 2007, San Francisco hosted a conference of Industrial Designers Society of America. Wanting to become designers and do something together, Joe and Brian thought of attending the conference. When they looked at the conference website, they realized all the hotel rooms were booked. By this time, they had run out of money and were unable to pay the rent of $1,150 per month. That's when a creative solution hit them! They had a lot of room in their apartment and no furniture, so they decided to rent the apartment for $80 a night to the guests of the conference. They arranged for a few airbeds and decided to make Pop-Tarts for breakfast. They quickly put up a site which was initially called 'Air Bed and Breakfast'. The idea worked. The first Airbnb guests were a 30-year-old Indian man, Amol; a 35-year-old woman from Boston, Katherine, and a 45-year-old father of four from Utah, Michael. So comfortable were the guests that they stayed for a week.

When they left, Joe and Brian realized that their idea could become something big—the idea was to make it possible for people to reserve someone's home the way one can reserve a hotel. Despite creating the company on a whim, they saw the potential to transform it into something meaningful, so they approached Harvard graduate and technical architect Nathan Blecharczyk, an ex-roommate of Joe's, to join the team as the third co-founder.

No idea is small. Just give it a try!

The company, however, wasn't able to get off its feet and ran into a debt of $40,000. For two years, Brian would wake up in a panic every morning and somehow convince himself throughout the day that what he was doing was right.

It was during this time of uncertainty that the Democratic National Convention was to begin. There was a housing crisis that had been talked about all over the news. Brian and Joe reached out to small bloggers and then slightly bigger bloggers and then the *Denver Post* and the *Rocky Mountain News* to write about their Airbnb story. Finally, they got on the local NBC news and even the *New York Times*. But they still had no business and no money. They launched on *Tech Crunch* in August 2008 to severe backlash and criticism. Some said it was the worst idea; others said they were serial killers!

Undeterred, they kept thinking about how to have a breakthrough. To repay their debt and build enough capital, they decided to create special edition cereals 'Obama O's' and 'Cap'n McCain's' based on the year's presidential candidates—Barack Obama and John McCain. Imagining they could get General Mills or Kellogg's to fill the boxes, they were in for a disappointment. No one returned their calls. The small cereal companies asked for $200,000. However, a fellow alumnus from RISD, who had a print shop, offered to print 1,000 boxes. They assembled the boxes in their apartments with hot glue, filled it with $1 cereals and mailed the boxes to press. With the publicity garnered, they managed to sell the boxes for $40 each and eventually earned $30,000, enough to almost get them out of debt. But the money didn't last long.

On the advice of well-wishers, they applied to Y Combinator. The interview with Paul Graham did not start off well as Graham asked, 'People are actually doing this? Why, what's wrong with them?' Just when the interview was over, Joe gave Graham a box each of the Obama O's and Cap'n McCain's. The survival story with cereals impressed Graham. 'Wow. You guys are like cockroaches. You just won't die,' he said.[7] A few days later, they were in Y Combinator and received $20,000 in funding.

*Never let criticism and obstacles deter
you from what you believe in.*

When Joe and Brian parted ways after their college graduation, Joe had said to Brian, 'Before you get on the plane, there's something I need to tell you. We're going to start a company one day, and they're going to write a book about it.'[8]

By March 2009, Airbnb had 2,500 listings and close to 10,000 registered users. More than 120,000 people used

---

[7] Leigh Gallagher, 'Airbnb's Surprising Path to Y Combinator', *Wired*, 21 February 2017. Available at https://www.wired.com/2017/02/airbnbs-surprising-path-to-y-combinator/; accessed on 15 March 2021.

[8] Avery Hartmans and Paige Leskin, 'The Rise of Airbnb CEO Brian Chesky, Who Got His Start Renting Out Air Mattresses on His Floor and Is Now Headed toward a Highly Anticipated IPO', *Business Insider*, 17 November 2020. Available at https://www.businessinsider.com/airbnb-ceo-brian-chesky-30-billion-startup-2016-8; accessed on 15 March 2021.

Airbnb during the 2014 FIFA World Cup. In 2015, Airbnb became an official sponsor of the 2016 Summer Olympics in Rio de Janeiro, Brazil. Today, Airbnb has more than five million unique places where people can stay in more than 81,000 cities and 191 countries.

Brian himself has come a long way. From an artist to a bodybuilder to a designer to now a CEO, he has worn many hats. Teaching himself about management through trial and error, Brian believes in 'going to the source' when a topic is to be learnt. This method helped him acquire a lot of mentors and well-wishers. One of his mentors even admitted, 'I wish I had thought of Airbnb.'[9] The man was no other than Warren Buffett!

> *Find good mentors who can teach you
> what you need to learn.*

But despite the success, Airbnb faced numerous crises. From racism and ransacking to burglary, sex scandals, murder and the recent effects of the pandemic, the company has seen it all. The American Hotel and Lodging Association asserted that they were receiving unfair competition from Airbnb, which resulted in additional regulations being imposed on the company. To top it all, many cities in the world, including some of the most popular Airbnb cities like New York and Paris, had strict laws about sharing homes and short-term rentals that affected their functioning and legal battles had to be fought to modify laws. A 24/7 customer support and a logistics and compliance team had to be built along with

---

[9]Leigh Gallagher, 'The Education of Airbnb's Brian Chesky', *Fortune*, 26 June 2015. Available at https://fortune.com/longform/brian-chesky-airbnb/; accessed on 15 March 2021.

local teams who were trained to manage the issues exclusive to each city.

The 2020 crisis had a direct impact on Airbnb with travel, especially recreational travel, coming to a standstill for months. Like most company heads, Brian too had to make the difficult decision of scaling down and letting go of almost a quarter of Airbnb's workforce. The company saw their business drop 80 per cent in eight weeks, but as a result of the discipline and optimism of its co-founder, it has managed to bounce back and survive the worst. The pandemic made Airbnb focus on their core home share business while pausing investments in other units of the company, such as transportation and hotels. However, with the new year, Brian has already begun to rehire some of the staff he had to let go. The 39-year-old's main focus is to build a high-quality company that prioritizes human connection over everything else. And it does seem like even the pandemic did not make him lose his spirit. The company now has a presence in 220 countries and Brian is ready to face the new redefined version of travel that has resulted from the pandemic. Airbnb's mantras to success have always been craziness, not editing one's imagination and a lot of hustle! 'The thing that will destroy Airbnb,' Brian said in an interview with *Fortune*, 'is if we stop being crazy.'[10]

Be crazy. Do not edit your imagination.

In the initial days, Silicon Valley was sceptical about this company because it was being set up by two designers from Art School, but the USP of Airbnb is that it is design driven.

---

[10]Leigh Gallagher, 'The Education of Airbnb's Brian Chesky', *Fortune*, 26 June 2015. Available at https://fortune.com/longform/brian-chesky-airbnb/; accessed on 15 March 2021.

In fact, its success can be attributed to the fact that every part of the trip is designed for the customer. The idea of designing a holistic experience for the customers came to Chesky from Walt Disney's movie *Snow White and the Seven Dwarfs*. Just like Walt Disney created storyboards, Airbnb storyboarded the perfect trip, frame by frame, for the customer. The emotional stories that described the complete Airbnb experience are what keep the company going. But the stories are not only those of the customer. There are stories of people being able to earn a livelihood because of Airbnb, new entrepreneurs growing because of Airbnb and lifelong friendships forming because of Airbnb.

One such story is of the first guests of Airbnb, Katherine and Amol. Katherine enjoyed the experience so much that she ended up moving to San Francisco from Boston and Amol invited Brian, Joe and Nathan to his wedding. It is these heart-to-heart connections that the company thrives on. Brian feels that a visitor experiences a city through its people, its Airbnb host. To Brian a city is not about its monuments and landmarks, but about the people. And that's what defines the culture of the company.

Stories like these have transformed Airbnb from a social experiment into a movement. In fact, welcoming strangers into his own home and going and living in a stranger's house himself, Brian admits, has made him a kinder and more generous person. Today, his company offers a programme that allows hosts to give free housing to refugees and relief workers and Brian himself has signed up to be a part of Warren Buffett and Bill and Melinda Gates's Giving Pledge project. He describes his motivation behind this on the Giving Pledge website: 'There is a saying that a great trip can set you down a path that doesn't end when you return. With this pledge, I want to help more kids realize the kind of journey I have had.'[11]

What make Brian so successful are his focus and his curiosity. Travelling the world with his partner, Elissa Patel—an artist he met on the dating app Tinder—Brian feels that travel is not about where you can go but who you can become and the memories you can make. His company, with its many product acquisitions and tie-ups, makes it possible for customers to book experiences where they not only live like locals but also have a local experience in order to create such life-transforming memories. Brian's goal is also geared towards enriching and strengthening the cities and neighbourhoods that they serve and, hence, it is no surprise that he was appointed a presidential ambassador for global entrepreneurship by President Obama in 2015.

In college, the young, dreamy-eyed art student had learnt that design is not about how something looks but about how something works. He had also learnt that it was possible to design the kind of world we want to live in—a motto he took to heart. With a company that believes that the future is built on human connections and thrives on diversity, trust and the goodness of people, Airbnb is truly Brian's greatest design project as it has helped create a world where not only him, but millions of others want to live.

You can design the kind of world you want to live in.

---

[11]https://givingpledge.org/Pledger.aspx?id=180; accessed on 15 March 2021.

Chapter 6

STARTING A REVOLUTION

Chad Hurley: Co-founder of YouTube

In early 2007, when a 12-year-old Canadian boy won second place at a local singing contest in Stratford, his mom uploaded some videos of her son singing on the video sharing website, YouTube, for family and close friends. The song gained a lot of popularity, so the mother continued uploading more and more videos. Soon, the boy's popularity on the site grew. Within days a music manager, Scooter Braun, discovered his videos and invited him to the US to record demo tapes. The boy is Justin Bieber and his journey since his first video on YouTube is the stuff dreams are made of.

When Chad Hurley, Steve Chen and Jawed Karim built YouTube, little did they know about the revolution they were creating and the impact it would have on the lives of people the world over. Chad, Jawed and Steve had been employees at PayPal. When PayPal was acquired by eBay for $1.54 billion, Chad left the company. He stayed in touch with his old friends, though, and they would often meet up for coffee. In one of their regular conversations, Chad shared his frustrations about the lack of a proper video sharing platform with Steve and Jawed. They all agreed that there was a need for such a platform where videos could be easily shared from their computers.

Legend has it that one winter in 2005, after a dinner party at Steve's San Francisco apartment, Chad and Steve had some trouble sharing the recordings of the party that they had made on a camcorder and digital camera with friends because of the massive file size. And that's when they thought of creating a video sharing website. However, like most companies, YouTube was probably not really founded in a single moment and actually evolved over many months. One of the early inspirations for YouTube could have even been the dating site HOTorNOT.com, where anyone could upload content that others could view. However, the concept was far too narrow, and YouTube turned out to be much, much more, with people posting whatever videos they wanted.

The three friends launched YouTube on 14 February 2005, from a little room above a pizza shop and a Japanese restaurant in San Mateo, California. The domain was registered for $20. The first video was uploaded on 23 April 2005. It was titled 'Me at the Zoo' and was a 19-second description of elephants by Jawed Karim at the San Diego Zoo. The video can still be found on their site today and has over 155 million views! Jawed soon left the company and decided to go back to Stanford. Steve and Chad continued with YouTube.

Convert your frustrations into actions.

Born to Donald Hurley, a financial consultant, and JoAnn, a school teacher, on 24 January 1977, Chad is the middle child with a younger brother, Brent, and an older sister, Heather. With a varied range of interests, Chad was no geeky child. At school, he ran track and cross country and was on two of the championship teams in 1992 and 1994 that won his school the Pennsylvania Interscholastic Athletic Association's state championship in boys' cross country. A part of the Technology Student Association while in Berks County's Twin Valley High School, in ninth grade, he built an amplifier that won him the third place in a national electronics competition. Though not really an academically oriented child, he was curious about a lot of things!

Chad had displayed a keen interest in arts ever since he was a child and spent a lot of his time water colouring and sculpting. Even while in elementary school, he displayed entrepreneurial instincts; he set up shop on the sidewalk outside his home where he sold his sketches and artwork. By the time he was in college, at Indiana University of Pennsylvania (IUP), he bought himself a Dell computer, converted a closet into a computer room and spent his time holed up inside exploring the web—which was quite new at the time—teaching himself HTML, studying web design, playing games and experimenting with animation. His inspiration was Walt Disney, who he describes as 'a true visionary'.[1]

In college, he switched to Fine Arts from Computer Science in the second semester, with a minor in print making. In college, too, he ran track and cross country all four years, his specialties being 1,500 metres and 800 metres. Putting his art and design skills to good use, he designed a runner with the IUP letters for cross country and track shirts. The emblem became so popular that it later showed up on t-shirts and even tattoos! His cross-country coach in IUP, Ed Fry, is quoted in *IUP Magazine* as saying, 'He was a good student. Very conscientious and kind of quiet and unassuming.' Shortly

---

[1]Courtney Trenwith, 'Meet the Man Who Created YouTube but What Did Chad Hurley Do Next?', *Arabian Business*, 8 November 2014. Available at https://www.arabianbusiness.com/meet-man-who-created-youtube-but-what-did-chad-hurley-do-next--570863.html; accessed on 15 March 2021.

before graduating, he had told Fry, 'You watch. I'm going to do something. You'll see.'[2]

And what he went on to do is create a revolution much bigger than even television. YouTube has over two billion monthly users worldwide. One billion hours of videos are watched daily on the site with over 720,000 hours of videos being uploaded daily.

Right out of college, where he earned a BA degree in Fine Arts in 1999, Chad read about the future launch of a new company called PayPal in the Science and Discoveries section of *Wired* magazine. They were looking for a web designer. He immediately sent an email to the company in Palo Alto, California, to find out whether they were offering any jobs. He also offered to design their logo for them. Soon after, he was hired as one of its first employees. His logo was adopted, and he became the official graphic designer for the company.

Talent never goes to waste.

The dotcom boom had already brought thousands of people to the Silicon Valley when Chad moved there to join PayPal. Finding a place to live was a big challenge, so Chad slept on the floor at a friend's house for a few weeks, borrowing money for pizza before he got his first pay cheque. He left PayPal after three-and-a-half years in 2002, soon after it was acquired by eBay. Being an early employee, he managed to walk away with a nice amount that allowed him to indulge in a few luxuries and even gave him plenty of leftover seed money for a future venture.

At the time of starting YouTube, the main motive was to solve a problem that the friends had encountered. The trio

---

[2]https://www.iup.edu/magazine/page.aspx?id=65161; accessed on 15 March 2021.

knew nothing about bandwidth and hosting and streaming issues. Chad said in an interview with *IUP Magazine*, 'None of us had any experience with it, but we could see there was a need to be able to share clips from cell phones and other places.'[3] Their first video to reach one million views was a Nike advertisement featuring Ronaldinho in November 2005. They tracked their success by calculating how many videos they could serve and how many views they were getting and when they reached one million, they realized they were onto something big.

Where there is a need, there is always a way.

YouTube quickly became one of the web's fastest growing sites and was ranked as the tenth most popular website just a year after its launch. Beginning as a venture capital-funded technology start-up, YouTube received an initial $3.5 million investment from Sequoia Capital—which has helped finance Apple, Google and other Valley greats—and an additional $8 million investment from Artis Capital Management and Sequoia Capital in April 2006.

By the summer of 2006, YouTube was recording 100 million video views per day. Chad said about YouTube in the same interview with *IUP Magazine*, 'We hoped we'd build a great business, and we feel fortunate to have a chance to do it again after PayPal. It has a lot to do with the environment of innovation we were surrounded by.'[4] YouTube made Chad and Steve famous in Silicon Valley almost immediately.

The pace at which YouTube was growing spiralled out of control. At the time, the company had only 67 employees,

---

[3] https://www.iup.edu/magazine/page.aspx?id=65161; accessed on 15 March 2021.
[4] https://www.iup.edu/magazine/page.aspx?id=65161; accessed on 15 March 2021.

including Chad and Steve. Despite having the required tools and processes in place, they often found themselves being threatened with lawsuits and copyright infringement issues, and were often struggling to deal with the enormous growing problems of the website by themselves. This was when Google offered to acquire YouTube—a relief for Chad and Steve. Chad spoke about the acquisition in an interview with *Arabian Business* magazine, 'If it was up to us, we would have liked the opportunity to stay independent and continue to create YouTube on our own, but unfortunately [because of] the forces of growth, the situation that we found ourselves in, that wasn't an option for us and Google, luckily for us, has provided the support and resources to take things to the next level.'[5] So, within 18 months of their launch, in November 2006, YouTube was sold to Google for $1.65 billion. Chad and Steve's video from the day that Google acquired YouTube is available for all to see on the site—and has four million views! The duo seemed very happy that their brainchild attracted the attention of the innovation giant. To Chad and Steve, Google and YouTube made sense together as their cultures were very similar.

It is okay to reach out for help.

Constantly thinking about the next challenge and how to solve the next problem is what kept Chad grounded, and selling to Google gave him the financial freedom and resources to pursue other creative projects. With Google, YouTube was really in great hands. Today, YouTube has an undeniable social impact,

---

[5]Courtney Trenwith, 'Meet the Man Who Created YouTube but What Did Chad Hurley Do Next?', *Arabian Business*, 8 November 2014. Available at https://www.arabianbusiness.com/meet-man-who-created-youtube-but-what-did-chad-hurley-do-next--570863.html; accessed on 15 March 2021.

has caused cultural changes and even provided a platform for politics. With the launch of YouTube Partner Program in 2007, people were able to turn their hobbies into businesses and create content that would reach millions around the world. Being a YouTuber is now a legitimate profession, and the number of channels that earn $10,000 per year on YouTube is growing by around 50 per cent every year.

Chad, however, seems unperturbed by the movement he has helped create. 'I just take everything on a day-to-day basis and try to pursue things that interest me, that I enjoy,' he says in the interview with *Arabian Business* magazine. Humbly, he adds, 'I feel really fortunate to have been in the right place at the right time to take advantage of these opportunities and hopefully I'll have the chance to create more solutions that people enjoy and use on a daily basis.'[6] With this pursuit in mind, he stepped down from the position of CEO of YouTube in 2010.

Above all, be humble.

In 2011, Steve and he went on to collaborate on building Avos Systems—an incubator that helped developers create apps in real time—along with Vijay Karunamurthy. The company is responsible for powering web and mobile applications MixBit, Delicious and Wanpai. But of all products, Chad's brainchild MixBit got the most attention. MixBit is an app that lets users record clips and create videos collaboratively, and stems from Chad's desire to create tools for people so that they can make better content. Being pragmatic, Chad doesn't dream

---

[6]Courtney Trenwith, 'Meet the Man Who Created YouTube but What Did Chad Hurley Do Next?', *Arabian Business*, 8 November 2014. Available at https://www.arabianbusiness.com/meet-man-who-created-youtube-but-what-did-chad-hurley-do-next--570863.html; accessed on 15 March 2021.

of duplicating YouTube's success. His goal never really was making a lot of money, but more about putting his ideas to work in order to make a difference and taking it a day at a time. MixBit also saw Chad and Steve going on their different paths for the first time in 15 years. MixBit had always been Chad's baby, so he took on the helm there; meanwhile, Steve moved over to Google Ventures. Steve said in an interview with *Tech Crunch*, 'Actually, it was a very personal and difficult decision to make, but with the decision to turn Avos into MixBit it became pretty clear. MixBit was Chad's idea before we started Avos and even at YouTube, and if I feel driven to work on other projects, then I'm just getting in the way of MixBit and the team.'[7] Chad joked, however, that he can always stop by Steve's and steal some food every once in a while. MixBit, now called Zeen, was acquired by BlueJeans in August 2018.[8] Perhaps, as you finish reading this, Chad would have moved on to his next venture: domain investing.

Even with CEO and co-founder of YouTube on his resume, Chad is not afraid to start anew with a new start-up. After all, as he mentions in an interview with *Bloomberg* to Emily Chang, in order to begin a start-up, you 'just have to be someone with ideas.'[9] Today, he is a part owner of the NBA's Golden

---

[7] Jordan Crook, 'YouTube Co-Founders Split as Hurley Spins Out MixBit and Chen Joins Google Ventures', *TechCrunch*, 6 June 2014. Available at https://techcrunch.com/2014/06/06/youtube-co-founders-break-up-as-chad-hurley-spins-out-his-own-company-and-steve-chen-joins-google-ventures/; accessed on 15 March 2021.

[8] Jordan Crook, 'YouTube Co-Founders Split as Hurley Spins out MixBit and Chen Joins Google Ventures', *TechCrunch*, 6 June 2014. Available at https://techcrunch.com/2014/06/06/youtube-co-founders-break-up-as-chad-hurley-spins-out-his-own-company-and-steve-chen-joins-google-ventures/; accessed on 15 March 2021.

[9] https://www.bloomberg.com/news/videos/2015-07-24/youtube-co-founder-

State Warriors and the Major League Soccer's Los Angeles Football Club, and is married to Kathy Clark, the daughter of James Clark, legendary Silicon Valley entrepreneur. For someone who created a sharing platform, which gives us an access to the lives of people all over the world, Chad himself is an intensely private person. His account on YouTube has no content, but around 4,830 subscribers. The world can be rest assured, though, that he will be churning out one creative venture after the other because as Hurley has exemplified through his creations, he wants to keep making a difference wherever he can.

> *Life is really not about sitting around,*
> *but about making a difference.*

---

chad-hurley-full-show-7-23-; accessed on 15 March 2021.

Chapter 7

SOLVING PROBLEMS

Drew Houston: Co-founder of Dropbox

The year was 2006. Drew Houston was on a Chinatown bus from Boston to New York and thought of getting some work done on the four-and-a-half-hour ride. He worked at a company called Accolade, which he had co-founded with one of his teachers. On opening his laptop, he noticed that he had left his thumb drive with all his work files at home. Frustrated and angry at himself for being disorganized and forgetful, Drew opened up his laptop and started frantically typing some Python code—he just had to find a solution to his problem.

The solution Drew thought of was a remote storage programme that users could access online to store their files from anywhere in the world. His main aim was to solve the storage problem, so that he would always have access to all his files. Within two weeks, he created a prototype and a demo video. The video made it to the front page of *Hacker News*—the news site owned by the start-up accelerator, Y Combinator. Drew, an avid reader, had read that the technique of putting up a video was successful in drawing attention to a product. It worked. Y Combinator's co-founder Paul Graham reached out to Drew and expressed an interest in his product. He had one condition: Drew needed to get a co-founder in order to be eligible for seed money. Paul Graham knew that new companies are far more likely to succeed if they have more than one founder, more than one person to make decisions and cope with the workload. Drew decided to fly down to San Francisco and talk to Graham in person and bounce some ideas off him, but Graham was visibly annoyed with Drew showing up unannounced and asked him to follow the conventional route and fill out the application first. Dejected, Drew returned to Boston. He had once applied to get into Y Combinator earlier with no success and did not want to lose his chance this time around.

Drew realized that getting a co-founder was his best bet. Meanwhile, somewhere in MIT, Drew's alma mater, a senior undergraduate studying Computer Science and Electrical Engineering, Arash Ferdowski, had seen Drew's demo video and reached out to him saying how awesome it was. Arash wanted to meet Drew and got introduced through a common friend. The two met up at the student centre at MIT and hit it off right away. The meeting lasted two hours, and Arash immediately decided to drop out of MIT and join Drew in his new venture. 'It was sort of like getting married on the first or second date,' Drew later said in an interview with *Business Insider*. 'It was wild because I thought I would have to, like, talk to his parents or somehow reassure him that this was a good decision to spend most of our waking hours for the foreseeable future together, but to his credit, he just jumped right in.'[1]

---

[1] Alyson Shontell and Anna Mazarakis, 'Dropbox Founder Reveals How He Built a $10 Billion Company in His 20s—Even Though Steve Jobs Told Him Apple Would Destroy It', *Business Insider*, 12 June 2017. Available at https://www.businessinsider.com/dropbox-founder-and-ceo-drew-houston-interview-2017-6/commerce-on-business-insider; accessed on 15 March 2021.

With the problem of a co-founder solved, Drew's company got accepted into Y Combinator. Drew settled on the name Dropbox for his company but found that Dropbox.com was already taken. So, in September 2007, after Arash and Drew decided to move to San Francisco to work on the company full time, they decided to drop in on the owner of the original Dropbox.com with a $20 bottle of wine. Although they were received well, the man refused to budge from his decision and change the name of his domain. When Drew's company went public, a lot of people confusedly went to Dropbox.com mistaking it to be Drew's company. To capitalize on the traffic, the owner of the domain put up a Google AdWords landing page on his site. According to Drew, the ads were for all of their competitors. Drew and Arash did some research on cyber trademark law and found that it was illegal for someone to intentionally confuse consumers. They decided to sue the owner of Dropbox.com for trademark infringement. This got the man's attention and he decided to sell the trademark Dropbox to Arash and Drew once the lawsuit was dropped. Drew offered him a choice of stock or $300k, but he chose to go with the money. Had he gone for stock, he would have been richer by hundreds of millions of dollars today—after all Dropbox is considered one of Y Combinator's most successful graduates, and today, has over 600 million users.

Finding a solution where there is a problem is often the best way to find success.

Born to Ken Houston, an engineer, and Cecily Houston, a high-school librarian, on 4 March 1983, Drew Houston grew up in Acton, Massachusetts. The Houston family owned an IBM PCjr and Drew was only two-and-a-half years old when he first started playing games on it. By five, his father taught him BASIC and he had already started programming. His entrepreneurial spirit kicked in early and when he was thirteen he was already saying he wanted to be the next Bill Gates! In sixth grade, when he expressed an interest in finding out how to form a company, his mother took him to the town hall to talk to a clerk. His passion was recognized even by his peers and it's not a surprise that on his high school yearbook at Acton-Boxborough Regional High School, he was voted as 'most likely to start a company'.[2]

What Drew found most interesting was breaking things apart and finding out how they worked or in certain cases why something did not work. Obsessed with gaming, he wanted to know how to make computer games. Once while beta testing a new computer game and realizing that it had security flaws, he confidently e-mailed the designer about it, who asked him if he could fix it for them. He was hired immediately! Only fourteen, Drew curiously asked his father, 'How old do I have to be to sign a contract?'[3] His parents had to sign all the paperwork and Drew got his first engineering gig. Soon, he started working for other local companies as well—like the industrial robotics start-up run by an MIT professor, for whom Drew converted their code to Linux.

Self-admittedly computer obsessed, Drew even took his computer gear on holidays with his family and set his monitors up for work wherever he went. Reverse engineering was his greatest passion and he was always curious as to how things

---

[2]https://podcastnotes.org/2018/08/30/dropbox/; accessed on 15 March 2021.
[3]Katia Savchuk, 'How to Raise a Billionaire: An Interview with Dropbox CEO Drew Houston's Parents', *Forbes*, 23 November 2015. Available at https://www.forbes.com/sites/katiasavchuk/2015/11/23/how-to-raise-a-billionaire-an-interview-with-dropbox-ceo-drew-houstons-parents/; accessed on 15 March 2021.

were made or how a problem could be solved. When invited to give MIT's 147th commencement address on 7 June 2013, Drew said, 'When I think about it, the happiest and most successful people I know don't just love what they do, they're obsessed with solving an important problem, something that matters to them.'[4]

Obsession is sometimes a good thing.

He finally started his own company—Accolade, a test prep company—at the age of 21, when he took a year off MIT, where he was studying Computer Science. Drew had scored a perfect score on his SATs and to help himself remember things and study, he created a software programme that made flashcards. This experience came in handy for Accolade, when he teamed up to work with a former high school teacher, Andrew Crick, in creating new online courses for the SATs.

Born in the restaurant Chilli's, this idea gave Drew firsthand experience into the workings of a business. He picked up card stock from Staples and created business cards that said 'Founder' on them, and went on Amazon and bought books on all the topics he felt he needed to learn about like sales, marketing, finance and products. Reading, he feels, is what provided him with a basic concept about different aspects of a business, and this held him in good stead later at Dropbox.

Dropbox got its first funding from Sequoia Capital. Drew recalls hitting 'Refresh' on the company's Bank of America checking account page online, and seeing it escalate in a moment from $60 to $1.2 million. Unable to believe this had

---

[4]http://news.mit.edu/2013/commencement-address-houston-0607; accessed on 15 March 2021.

really happened, Drew, then aged 24, made his first purchase at the electronic store Radio Shack for $17.35!

The company publicly launched its service in 2008, a year after getting funding from Sequoia. Before its launch, it faced a lot of criticism. One of the main arguments against it was that similar ideas had already been tried. Many investors even asked Drew why he had created a storage company when there were already many like it. Drew often asked in return: yes, but do you use any of them? Not believing in the myth that one had to come up with a novel idea or be first in the market to succeed, Drew read about the success of other companies and pulled strength from their failures and struggles. He discovered that in most cases, the breakout success stories were of companies that had some form of predecessors: Google was preceded by Yahoo, Alta Vista, Ask Jeeves, and many other search engines. Facebook was preceded by Myspace, Orkut, and Friendster.

You don't have to be the first to solve a problem;
you simply have to be the best at it.

Drew and Arash took their time to make sure their product was working all right before the launch. To attract its first customers, they put up promotional videos on discussion websites such as Reddit and Slashdot so that technology sector influencers could use it and speak positively about the product. They hoped that this would result in word-of-mouth promotion and user numbers would grow. The method worked, and from 5,000 users on a waiting list, within a few days, Dropbox had 75,000 sign ups. Then it went from 100,000 users to 200,000 users in 10 days. User numbers soared even faster when they came up with an incentivized referral scheme where they offered existing Dropbox customers more free storage space if they could get a friend to sign up. This attracted many new customers and in 2011, Dropbox grabbed the attention of Steve Jobs, Apple's CEO at the time, who expressed an interest to buy Dropbox and make it a part of Apple. But Drew refused, a decision that he admits now didn't seem to go down all that well with Jobs. Dropbox also caught the attention of Facebook founder, Mark Zuckerberg. Zuckerberg sent Drew a message over Facebook, which Drew mistook to be a prank.

What motivates Drew to keep improving on his product, aside from his obsession to solve a problem, are personal experiences and emails from people who write in to say that Dropbox has made collaborating easier and has helped them start a music festival, or make a movie, or even launch the company they had been dreaming of. Drew has proven that making an impact is possible even when faced with obstacles. At the MIT commencement address, Drew also said, 'Failure doesn't matter, you only have to be right once.'[5]

The CEO of Dropbox by 24 years of age, Drew said in the interview with *Business Insider*, 'No one is born a CEO. This is an acquired skill set, and, furthermore, it's one that you learn on the job. So everyone is a first-time CEO by definition at some point.' Recalling that he learnt almost everything about the job from the books he kept reading and also from helpful mentors who owned start-ups, he added, 'just about everything is learnable.'[6]

---

[5]http://news.mit.edu/2013/commencement-address-houston-0607; accessed on 15 March 2021.

[6]Alyson Shontell and Anna Mazarakis, 'Dropbox Founder Reveals How He Built a $10 Billion Company in His 20s—Even Though Steve Jobs Told Him Apple Would Destroy It', *Business Insider*, 12 June 2017. Available at https://www.businessinsider.com/dropbox-founder-and-ceo-drew-houston-interview-2017-6/

2020 turned out to be another year of learning for Drew, as with most other business owners. With most work going online, customers relied more on Dropbox for sharing data and storing their content safely. This opened up the opportunity for Drew to introduce a number of new features, adapt to the new environment where lines between home and work have blurred and design new tools that could help his customers adjust to the new distributed work system. So, even with the difficulties the world faced last year, Drew's company stayed profitable and successful. That is perhaps because, even through it all, he kept focusing on the evolving needs of his customers and how he could better solve them.

In 2013, at the commencement speech at MIT, standing in the rain, facing a crowd of eager students about to graduate, the 30-year-old Drew admitted that he never really had a grand plan for his life. All he did was to find a solution to a problem he faced, a problem he thought everyone was facing. And Dropbox happened! Towards the end of his motivating speech, he recalled how his 95-year-old grandmother would always end their phone conversations with one word: 'Excelsior'[7]—and that's exactly how Drew and Dropbox have grown—forever upward.

You can learn almost anything
if you put your heart into it.

---

commerce-on-business-insider; accessed on 15 March 2021.
[7]http://news.mit.edu/2013/commencement-address-houston-0607; accessed on 15 March 2021.

Chapter 8

REACHING FOR THE STARS

*Elon Musk: Co-founder of PayPal,
Founder of Tesla and SpaceX*

While preparing for the role of Tony Stark, aka Iron Man, Robert Downey Jr thought it would be a good idea to sit down and have a chat with Elon Musk. He said, 'This is a guy who can give us some insight into what it'd really be like to be Tony Stark.'[1] Elon Musk is as close to Tony Stark as we can get in reality. Like the fictional Tony Stark of the Marvel series, Musk too is a technological entrepreneur who has changed the world with his revolutionary ideas. Probably the only person to have headed four billion-dollar companies—PayPal, Tesla, SpaceX, and Solar City—Elon Musk's ideas are often so grand that they are met with scepticism and disbelief. Musk's ideas are ambitious and often bordering on incredulous because he is a futurist who believes in the absolute necessity of technological advancement in order to help improve the future. 'When something is important enough, you do it even if the odds

---

[1] Eric Johnson, 'SpaceX CEO Elon Musk Has Done the "Real" Iron Man Several Favors', *Vox*, 12 October 2016. Available at https://www.vox.com/2016/10/12/13259344/elon-musk-iron-man-jon-favreau-tony-stark-spacex-recode-podcast; accessed on 15 March 2021.

are not in your favour,' he said in an interview with *CBS News*.[2]

> *If something is important, you should pursue it
> even if the odds are against you.*

Most of Musk's ideas have been revolutionary and way ahead of their times. Even as a child, Elon was often found lost in daydreaming about possible inventions, oblivious to what was going on around him. The doctors suspected that he was hard of hearing because he didn't respond when spoken to and even ordered for his adenoid glands to be removed. In a 2015 biography of Elon Musk by Ashlee Vance, his mother Maye admits, 'He goes into his brain and then you just see he is in another world. He still does that. Now I just leave him be because I know he is designing a new rocket or something.'[3]

Musk has done much more than just design a rocket, though. He is the founder of Space Exploration Technologies Corporation or SpaceX, the first private company to send its own rocket to the international space station. Elon launched this company in 2002, with the objective of eventually making commercial space travel possible. By September 2017, he presented a plan for the Big Falcon Rocket or the BFR, a gigantic 31-engine machine topped by a spaceship that would be able to carry at least 100 people to Mars as early as 2024. He calls the rocket the Starship now. Musk himself wants to be one of the first people to go to Mars and famously even said in a 2013 interview with *Vanity Fair*, 'I've said I want to

---

[2]Scott Pelley, 'U.S., China, Russia, Elon Musk: Entrepreneur's "Insane" Vision Becomes Reality', *CBS News*, 22 May 2012. Available at https://www.cbsnews.com/news/us-china-russia-elon-musk-entrepreneurs-insane-vision-becomes-reality/; accessed on 15 March 2021.

[3]Ashlee Vance, *Elon Musk: How the Billionaire CEO of SpaceX and Tesla is Shaping our Future* (2016, Random House).

die on Mars, just not on impact.'[4]

Musk strongly believes that in order to help our species survive and sustain, we must colonize Mars and be able to make life multi-planetary. Speaking at South by Southwest (SXSW) once, Musk said that in the event of a Third World War, and if we were to ever enter the Dark Ages, we would want to ensure that 'there's enough of a seed of human civilization somewhere else to bring it back and shorten the length of the dark ages.'[5] Of course, whether or not Mars can support human life is an ongoing scientific investigation, but Musk truly believes that it can be made possible and has often spoken of his ideas of how to transform Mars into a habitable planet. 'You want to be inspired by things. You want to wake up in the morning and think the future is going to be great. And that's what being a spacefaring civilization is all about. It's about believing in the future and thinking that the future will be better than the past. And I can't think of anything more exciting than going out there and being among the stars,' Musk says.[6]

Work towards building a better future.

In an anecdote he often mentions in interviews, Musk recalls how once, when he was on a date, the first question he asked

---

[4]Elien Blue Becque, 'Elon Musk Wants to Die on Mars', *Vanity Fair*, 10 March 2013. Available at https://www.vanityfair.com/news/tech/2013/03/elon-musk-die-mars; accessed on 15 March 2021.

[5]*LiveMint*, 'Space Bases Could Preserve Civilization in World War III: Elon Musk', 13 March 2018. Available at https://www.livemint.com/Science/zQdDv1iuJbZlmWXd0cchmL/Space-bases-could-preserve-civilization-in-World-War-III-El.html; accessed on 15 March 2021.

[6]Catherine Clifford, 'Elon Musk Defends Plans to Build a Community on Mars after Downbeat NASA Report', *CNBC*, 2 August 2018. Available at https://www.cnbc.com/2018/08/02/elon-musk-defends-plans-to-build-community-on-mars-after-nasa-report.html; accessed on 15 March 2021.

was, 'Do you ever think about electric cars?'[7] Musk joined the electric car company Tesla, founded in 2003 by entrepreneurs Martin Eberhard and Marc Tarpenning, at its Series A funding in 2004 and has led the company ever since. Tesla is dedicated to producing mass-market electric cars with the models S, X, Y and 3 cars already on the road, and work is in progress for the new Roadster and Semi, among others. Tesla's vehicles, which are known for their speed, are primarily aimed towards helping the world transition to sustainable energy by commercializing electric vehicles. In 2013, Musk proposed the idea of building an alternate form of transportation called the Hyperloop, which, powered by renewable energy, will carry passengers in pods through a network of low-pressure tubes at speeds reaching more than 1,200 km/h.

Aware of the suspicion that his ground-breaking ideas face daily, Musk says, 'If you go back a few hundred years, what we take for granted today would seem like magic—being able to talk to people over long distances, to transmit images, flying, accessing vast amounts of data like an oracle. These are all things that would have been considered magic a few hundred years ago.'[8] Many of Musk's ideas have clearly come from the books he has grown up with.

Born to Errol Musk, an engineer, and Maye Musk, a model and nutritionist in Pretoria, South Africa, on 28 June 1971, Elon, the oldest of three siblings, by his own admission, had a difficult childhood. Throughout his childhood, and especially

---

[7] Ashlee Vance, *Elon Musk: Tesla, SpaceX, and the Quest for a Fantastic Future* (2015, Ecco).

[8] Hannah Elliott, 'At Home with Elon Musk: The (Soon-to-Be) Bachelor Billionaire', *Forbes*, 26 March 2012. Available at https://www.forbes.com/sites/hannahelliott/2012/03/26/at-home-with-elon-musk-the-soon-to-be-bachelor-billionaire/#6f851884729b; accessed on 15 March 2021.

through his parent's divorce when he was only 9, books played an important part in engaging and entertaining him. In an interview in *Rolling Stone* magazine, Musk said, 'I was raised by books. Books, and then my parents.'[9]

The best ideas come from books.

After his parent's divorce, Elon decided to live with his father, a decision he regrets now, as his father, he admits, was not a nice person. Later, in the interview in *Rolling Stone* magazine, Elon had said that he had come to terms with the fact that he would not share a typical relationship with his father: 'In my experience, there is nothing you can do. Nothing, nothing. I wish. I've tried everything. I tried threats, rewards, intellectual arguments, emotional arguments, everything to try to change my father for the better, and he... no way, it just got worse.' Coupled with the emotional trauma at home was the bullying Elon faced regularly at school, which made his childhood brutal and extremely lonely. While describing the experience, Elon says, 'That's what made growing up difficult. For a number of years there was no respite.'[10]

For young Elon, technology was his only refuge and escape. When Elon first discovered a computer—the Commodore VIC-20—at the age of 10, he relentlessly urged his father to get him one. In three days straight, without sleep, he learned how to use the machine. 'It seemed like the most super-compelling

---

[9]Neil Strauss, 'Elon Musk: The Architect of Tomorrow', *Rolling Stone*, 15 November 2017. Available at http://www.rollingstone.com/culture/features/elon-musk-inventors-plans-for-outer-space-cars-finding-love-w511747; accessed on 15 March 2021.

[10]Ashlee Vance, *Elon Musk: Tesla, SpaceX, and the Quest for a Fantastic Future* (2015, Ecco).

thing I had ever seen,' he recalled later.[11] Teaching himself how to programme, he sold his first software at the age of 12 for $500—a science-fiction-inspired space game he created called Blastar.

The entrepreneurship bug bit Elon and his younger brother Kimbal early on. When Elon was 16, the duo tried to open a video arcade near their school, but they were stopped because they didn't have a real-estate permit. Their parents didn't take too well to the idea either.

At the time, 18-year-olds in South Africa were forced into joining the military, whose main duty was enforcing apartheid. Elon, in order to avoid being enrolled in the military and to study further, decided to move to Canada. He attended Queen's University and obtained his Canadian citizenship. Soon after, in 1992, he moved to the US—which he felt had always been at the forefront of all technological innovations—to study Business and Physics at the University of Pennsylvania. He graduated with two undergraduate degrees, in Economics and Physics. After his graduation, in 1995, he got admitted into the PhD programme in Energy Physics at Stanford University. But within two days, he dropped out to become a part of the Internet boom and jointly launched, with his brother, his very first company, Zip2 Corporation. An online city guide with maps for newspapers, Zip2 was bought over in 1999 by a division of Compaq Computer Corporation for $307 million in cash and $34 million in stock options.

Musk's first big company was X.com, an online payment platform. Musk invested some of his money from the Zip2 sale in the company. The next year, Confinity, whose online

---

[11] Ashlee Vance, *Elon Musk: Tesla, SpaceX, and the Quest for a Fantastic Future* (2015, Ecco).

payment platform was called PayPal, merged with X.com. The merged company continued operating their payment platform under the name PayPal, which was sold to eBay for $1.5 billion in stock in 2002. Musk earned $165 million from the sale.

In Olivia Tomlinson's book about him, Musk states, 'Going from PayPal, I thought: "Well, what are some of the other problems that are likely to most affect the future of humanity?"'[12] He did not think 'what's the best way to make money?' So he pooled all his money and resources into working towards the future and forming Tesla and SpaceX. As a young enthusiastic entrepreneur, Musk had said in 1999, 'I want to be on the cover of *Rolling Stone* ... that'd be cool!'[13] In 2017, he was! In his interview in *Rolling Stone*, he said, 'I try to do useful things. That's a nice aspiration. And useful means it is of value to the rest of society. Are they useful things that work and make people's lives better, make the future seem better, and actually are better, too? I think we should try to make the future better.'[14]

Do something that is useful.

Musk is averse to taking vacations and often works 120 hours a week; his ideas are unstoppable and so is he. Known for announcing a number of his new ventures on Twitter, on 17 December 2006 at 5.06 a.m., he tweeted: 'Traffic is driving

---

[12] Olivia Tomilson, *Elon Musk: Life Lessons with Billionaire CEO & Successful Entrepreneur—How Elon Musk is Innovating the Future* (2018, Cascade Publishing).
[13] https://www.marketwatch.com/story/elon-musk-gets-what-elon-musk-wants-just-watch-this-classic-video-from-1999-2019-01-28; accessed on 15 March 2021.
[14] Shawn Langlois, 'Elon Musk Gets What Elon Musk Wants, Just Watch This Classic Video from 1999', *Rolling Stone*, 28 January 2019. Available at http://www.rollingstone.com/culture/features/elon-musk-inventors-plans-for-outer-space-cars-finding-love-w511747; accessed on 15 March 2021.

me nuts. Am going to build a tunnel boring machine and just start digging...' He followed this up with a determined tweet at 8.17 am: 'I am actually going to do this.'[15] Immediately after, he launched The Boring Company, a company devoted to building tunnels in order to reduce street traffic. A test dig was carried out on the SpaceX property in Los Angeles and the company currently has a project under construction in Las Vegas to ferry people around the Las Vegas Convention Center campus.

When interviewing candidates for any of his companies, Musk, in order to find out if employees share a similar work ethic, is known to ask one question in particular: 'Tell me the story of your life and the decisions that you made along the way and why you made them and also tell me about some of the most difficult problems you worked on and how you solved them.'[16] His own life, his fears for the future and the challenges he faces daily have paved the way for all his technological endeavours. One of the issues he admits losing sleep over is the possibility of humanity getting supplanted by artificial intelligence, which Musk feels is even more of a threat to humanity than nuclear weapons. Therefore, he has devoted a lot of his time, money and expertise to saving the future from what he thinks are the wrong kind of robots. He became the co-founder and initial co-chair of the non-profit organization OpenAI, started in 2015, which works towards advancing digital intelligence to benefit humanity. Musk strongly believes

---

[15]Elon Musk (@elonmusk), 'Traffic Is Driving Me Nuts', *Twitter*, 17 December 2016. Available at https://twitter.com/elonmusk/status/810108760010043392?lang=en; accessed on 15 March 2021.

[16]Arjun Kharpal, 'How to Get Hired by Elon Musk', *CNBC*, 13 February 2017. Available at https://www.cnbc.com/2017/02/13/how-to-get-hired-by-elon-musk-job-interview.html; accessed on 15 March 2021.

that the only way to prevent artificial intelligence from taking over human lives is to integrate humans and machines. He feels so passionately about this that it is often referred to as Elon's crusade. In order to make this possible, he co-founded a venture called Neuralink, a neuro-technological company that aims to not only treat serious brain diseases but also create devices to be implanted in the human brain in order to create mind–computer interfaces and eventually make human enhancement possible.

As a father of six, Elon has even started his own school called Ad Astra, which focuses on catering to each individual student's capabilities, making them innovative and creative and preparing them for the technologically changing world. The school, housed in the SpaceX complex, trains the young generation for a future where they might have multi-planetary life. As the Latin phrase *ad astra* suggests, Elon dreams of reaching the stars and beyond. His dreams keep getting bigger and bigger, and he keeps turning impossibility into possibility and making the ludicrous a reality. With his innovations, he has already disrupted aerospace, telecommunications, energy, artificial intelligence, transportation, health and automotive industries, to name a few. With each venture he embarks upon, Musk helps us stretch our imagination and believe in possibilities unheard of before. Many of the technological changes we see in today's world are thanks to his vision. He aptly summed it up in an interview: 'When I was in college, I wanted to be involved in things that would change the world. Now I am.'[17]

To make big things happen, you must dream big.

---

[17] Levi Tillemann, *The Great Race: The Global Quest for the Car of the Future* (2015, Simon & Schuster).

Chapter 9

DARING TO BE DIFFERENT

Evan Spiegel: Founder of Snapchat

In 2012, while walking on stage in his cap and gown and waving at his family sitting in the audience at his graduation at Stanford, Evan Spiegel felt it was all a farce. Evan was not graduating. He was only 'faux graduating' as he was still a few credits short. Stanford allowed students who would be using the summer term to complete their degrees the alternative to walk on stage just like the rest. Evan did it because he wanted to conform and didn't want to feel embarrassed and left out. A few years later, at a commencement speech given to the class of 2015 at the University of Southern California's (USC's) Marshall School of Business, Spiegel said, 'Conforming happens so naturally that we can forget how powerful it is—we want to be accepted by our peers—we want to be a part of the group. It's in our biology. But the things that make us human are those times we listen to the whispers of our soul and allow ourselves to be pulled in another direction.'[1]

But by the time of Evan's faux graduation, he had already stopped conforming in many ways. Evan, along with college mates Bobby Murphy and Reggie Brown, had come up with

---
[1] https://www.youtube.com/watch?v=-Ng0fXIITt0&feature=emb_title; accessed on 15 March 2021.

an app that would make photos and videos disappear within minutes of sending them. The idea allegedly originated in a Stanford dorm room when Reggie complained to Evan about a photograph he had regretted sending and they wondered if it could be made to disappear somehow.

Originally named Picaboo, the app did not get off to a very good start. Launched in July 2011 on the iOS operating system, it fell short of expectations with only 127 users by the end of summer. A number of people thought it was a joke. Even venture capitalists, who were pitched the idea, had lukewarm reactions to it. By this time, fallout with Reggie Brown resulted in him being ousted from the trio. By September that year, the app had been rebranded and was called Snapchat. Within a year, by November 2012, users had shared over one billion photos on the Snapchat iOS app, with 20 million photos being shared per day.

You can achieve more if you do not conform.

Today, the company's profile states: 'We contribute to human progress by empowering people to express themselves, live in the moment, learn about the world and have fun together.'[2] What is most important to Evan is that in a world ruled by social networking, where young people are constantly under stress to look, be or behave in a certain way, Snapchat gives people an opportunity to be themselves. It encourages all of its users to be content creators; that is probably why when you open the app, it directly leads to the camera. In an interview with *Recode* in 2014, Evan said, 'It's about building something with feelings.'[3]

---

[2] https://www.snap.com/en-US/; accessed on 15 March 2021.
[3] Kurt Wagner, 'Inside Evan Spiegel's Very Private Snapchat Story', *Vox*, 9 May

To Evan, Snapchat is also about building deeper relationships with people we are close to. With its emphasis on maintaining a small group of friends, its philosophy runs counter to that of traditional social media. In fact, that was one of the reasons why when Facebook founder Mark Zuckerberg offered Spiegel $3 billion in cash to acquire Snapchat in 2013, he turned it down. Instead, he opted to grow his company on his own terms. Incidentally, Zuckerberg tried to acquire Spiegel's company, which is known as Snap Inc. again in 2016. At the commencement speech, Evan admitted, 'I am now convinced that the fastest way to figure out if you are doing something truly important to you is to have someone offer you a bunch of money to part with it.'[4]

Always work on your own terms.

Born to two illustrious attorneys, John W. Spiegel and Melissa Ann Thomas, on 4 June 1990 in California, Evan is the oldest of three children and has two sisters, Lauren and Caroline. The children grew up with money and privilege. Evan drove a Cadillac Escalade to his high school, the Crossroads School for the Arts and Sciences, and it is said that once he even blackmailed his parents into buying him a BMW. Yet, despite his moneyed roots, he believes that if one is in a position of privilege, one should own up to it. He has also not been shy to admit that when it came to the founding of his start-up, he really got lucky and just found ways in which he could make the most of his privilege.

The young Evan seems to be a study in contradictions. He

2016. Available at https://www.vox.com/2016/5/9/11594144/evan-spiegel-snapchat; accessed on 15 March 2021.
[4]https://www.youtube.com/watch?v=-Ng0fXIITt0&feature=emb_title; accessed on 15 March 2021.

is the nerd who built his first computer in sixth grade and also the party lover who met the co-founders of Snap at the Kappa Sigma fraternity party. He is the fashionista (incidentally, he met his wife, supermodel Miranda Kerr at a dinner for Louis Vuitton) who has appeared on the cover of *Vogue* and is also someone who is often seen wearing plain white T-shirts. He is the pragmatic person who lived with his father even after becoming a millionaire in order to save some money but is also the one who got the set designer of the hit TV show *Friends*, Greg Grande, to design his first house in Brentwood!

Despite the privileged upbringing, TV was not allowed in Spiegel house, and Evan was always encouraged by his parents to try new things. He recalls how once when he was in second grade, he wanted to learn to play the trumpet and his parents immediately signed him up for it. Another interest that he thought of trying out was design. While still in high school, he enrolled at the Otis College of Art and Design. This became a life changer for him as he fell in love with design. He pursued this passion further by attending classes at the Art Center College of Design in Pasadena, California. After graduating from high school, it was clear to him what he wanted to study, and he enrolled at Stanford to study product design.

Evan knew ever since he was a child that he wanted to start a company. When he saw his dad getting called into work and having to cancel family vacations, that's when he had decided that he wanted to be the guy on the phone when he grew up. He ended up becoming a successful entrepreneur at 21 and the world's youngest billionaire at 25.

Snapchat was, however, not Evan's first business idea. During his sophomore year at the Stanford, where he was enrolled to study product design, he got the chance to sit in on a class in the Stanford Graduate School of Business called 'Entrepreneurship and Venture Capital'. He met many entrepreneurs and CEOs who were visiting speakers in the class. At one such class, he met Scott Cook, the CEO of Intuit. After class, Spiegel claimed he begged Cook for a job at Intuit. Soon he was put into a three-people team who were making text-based applications for users in India. It was at that time that the thought struck Spiegel that if he could be a part of a small team and build really big things that could impact people across the globe, why did he need to do it at a big company? Spiegel teamed up with his friend Bobby, who lived across the hall from him, and they started working on several different projects.

One of their big projects was called 'Future Freshman', a website designed to help children get into college and deal with the stressful college admissions process. But the project never took off. Neither Bobby's brother nor Spiegel's sister, who were both applying to colleges, ever used it. Even though they had spent over a year and a half working on the project day and night, Evan and Bobby were able to learn a lesson from their failure. They decided to focus on projects with a simpler concept.

Failures and mistakes are no strangers to Evan. At the commencement speech at USC, Evan said, 'You are going to make a lot of mistakes. I've already made a ton of them—some of them very publicly—and it will feel terrible, but it will be okay. Just apologize as quickly as you can and pray for forgiveness.'[5] But according to Evan, what helped him truly grow was being able to access and learn from generous, smart people who taught him how to be a better leader. His

---

[5] https://www.youtube.com/watch?v=-Ng0fXIITt0&feature=emb_title; accessed on 15 March 2021.

advice to young people who want to become entrepreneurs is to meet as many people as they can and take up any and every job opportunity with them for free in order to learn more and more.

Say yes to every job opportunity in order to learn more.

Evan himself has always been curious to learn. Never ashamed to approach people and request for opportunities to work and learn, he bagged an internship position at Red Bull while in high school. He got a summer job doing early-stage computational drug discovery in pretty much the same way—by approaching people and telling them that he would do whatever they needed him to do. His curiosity and always-ready-to-learn spirit got him into design. After building his own computer as a child, he started playing around with Photoshop. Realizing his interest in design, he took a few graphic design classes in high school and even designed the school newspaper. Others often came to him with requests for designing their websites and T-shirts. Even to this day, he admits that designing is the favourite part of his work at Snap Inc. and he still gets to do it two to three times a week.

Spiegel's personality is reflected in many of Snapchat's attributes. A very private person, Evan has adopted this approach in his business too and believes strongly that users should be allowed to retain their own privacy. Unlike many other social networking sites, Snapchat doesn't ask users for too much personal information and doesn't target users with personal and personalized ads after collecting their private data. Spiegel's emphasis on loyalty and authenticity are reflected in the app's attribute of letting users interact and express themselves to people who are only in their trusted circle of friends. Snapchat works differently from most platforms available in the market. Private messages get auto deleted after they're read. Videos can be recorded and watched vertically and not horizontally. It is also in keeping with the company philosophy that Evan often feels the need to make design changes to the app. The changes are sometimes accepted well by the audience and sometimes not, but Evan's primary concern is not chasing high GDP which will demonstrate a high market value or growth of the company. He knows his mind and has strong conviction in the decisions he needs to make to uphold his company's value system. In an interview with the *Wall Street Journal*, Evan said, 'What's interesting about Snap's design process is it starts with people. We are trying to design around our values.'[6] That is probably why Snapchat stays away from typical social media concepts like public likes and comments; Evan feels it can make a person feel judged all the time. In the competitive market of social networking, this is what sets his products apart. Evan is certain about one thing—Snapchat is not a social site; it is a site for communication, with access to entertainment on the side.

Today, Snapchat has a number of features and is constantly adding more to keep its loyal customer base engaged. In 2019, the company unveiled Snap Games, a live multiplayer gaming platform. The company also added augmented-reality features to its Snapchat platform and expanded a line of original shows made exclusively for its audience. It also provides its users with news through a feature called Discover. Snapchat now has 265 million daily active users. The app is so popular among Gen Z that they are now often referred

---

[6]Georgia Wells and Matt Murray, 'Evan Spiegel Stands by the Big Bet that Sank Snap's Stock', *Wall Street Journal*, 2 November 2019. Available at https://www.wsj.com/articles/evan-spiegel-stands-by-the-big-bet-that-sank-snaps-stock-11572667238; accessed on 15 March 2021.

to as the 'Snapchat Generation'. With the pandemic, its user base has increased. During the pandemic, Snapchat became an extremely important tool to help people stay close to each other emotionally. By late March 2020, communication between Snapchat users was higher by more than 30 per cent as compared to the last week of January. From merely being a site for communication, Snapchat evolved into an important tool for disseminating life-saving information during the crisis by partnering with the World Health Organization and the Centers for Disease Control and Prevention in the US. Today, Evan feels it is much more than a site for communication and entertainment.

Evan is no longer the Stanford student who would conform to avoid embarrassment. After the birth of his son, Hart, with wife Miranda Kerr, he went back to Stanford to finish his degree. He wants to set a good example for his son. He no longer wants to blend in and be like his peers; he stands out, nonchalant and unapologetic, doing what his intuition tells him to do. In an interview with *Recode*, he sums up his motto: 'When you are working on a project that you feel passionate about, you can't let other people's doubts slow you down. Someone will always have an opinion about you. Whatever you do won't ever be enough. So find something important to you. Find something that you love.'[7]

Find something that is valuable to you, that you love doing,
And don't let other people's doubts slow you down.

---

[7] Kurt Wagner, 'Inside Evan Spiegel's Very Private Snapchat Story', *Vox*, 9 May 2016. Available at https://www.vox.com/2016/5/9/11594144/evan-spiegel-snapchat; accessed on 15 March 2021.

Chapter 10

IMAGINING THE IMPOSSIBLE

Larry Page: Co-founder of Google

In a commencement speech given at University of Michigan in 2009, a young man said, 'I have a story about following dreams. Or maybe more accurately, it's a story about finding a path to make those dreams real.'[1]

The man was Lawrence (Larry) Page and, one night, while still a student at Stanford University, he dreamt of the idea that led to Google! The story goes that he was struck in the middle of the night with a vision that he could download the entire web and just keep the links. He immediately wrote down his idea, absolutely convinced he could make it work within a few weeks.

Larry was only 22: an idealist and an optimist.

His academic advisor at Stanford, Terry Winograd, didn't want to burst his bubble and discourage his enthusiasm. He encouraged Larry to explore the idea further and when Page was dabbling in topics for his thesis, had even suggested that he work on the web for some time. Following his advisor's guidelines, Page decided to focus on how to optimize web-based searches for his dissertation. He felt no one was really

---

[1] https://www.youtube.com/watch?time_continue=7&v=qFb2rv mrahc&feature=emb_logo; accessed on 15 March 2021.

looking at how pages are linked on the web. Linking the pages was quite a task at the time, since there were at least 10 million documents floating about. Larry collaborated with Sergey Brin, a senior at Stanford, to build an algorithm that took into account the number and quality of links to a web page in order to get an idea of how important the website is. Named after Page, the algorithm was called PageRank.

At the time, the duo's work was mainly speculative as they didn't envision creating a search engine, but Larry's curiosity with backlinks led them to work on a project that analysed how web pages connected to one another through backlinks. A search engine was created in August 1996 called BackRub.

Be optimistic. Be curious.

The idea of the search engine seemed to work. The duo's lab was Larry's dorm and their computer was cobbled together out of spare parts and Lego bricks. Everything seemed to work, but for the name. Since the search engine was intended to index an unfathomable number of Internet web pages, a friend, Sean Anderson, suggested an alternate name—Googolplex. Larry preferred the shorter form Googol—the mathematical term that stands for 10—and according to their thesis, fit 'well with our goal of building very large-scale search engines'.[2] While checking for the availability of the domain name online, a typing error accidentally led Googol to become Google, thus leading to the birth of 'google.com'.

In a 1999 video of an unconventional-looking all-staff meeting of the start-up, Larry and Sergei's banter and friendship is visible. Sergei says that with Larry being the CEO and all, he should get a new throne and presents him with a chair.

---

[2] https://www.google.com/doodles/googles-21st-birthday; accessed on 15 March 2021.

Their obvious camaraderie developed late, though, as Larry and Sergei were far from friendly at their very first meeting at Stanford. Legend has it that they disagreed on almost everything during their first encounter when Sergey Brin was assigned to show Larry Page around the Stanford campus.

Before deciding to study at Stanford, Larry studied at the University of Michigan from where he got his BSc degree in Computer Engineering. Born in East Lansing, Michigan, on 26 March 1973, to Carl, a Computer Science professor, and Gloria, a school teacher who taught programming, Page had computing built into his DNA. His parents had also met at the University of Michigan. 'I grew up in a messy house. There were computers, gadgets, and tech magazines everywhere. I remember spending a lot of time reading,' Page said about his childhood.[3] When he was six, his parents got a home computer, the Exidy Sorcerer; his brother wrote an operating system for it and Larry used it to type his homework assignment, becoming the first student in his school to do so.

The creative and scientific environment that Larry grew up in is evident from his father's valedictory speech from Flint Mandeville High School, class of 1956, which Larry found later. In it, Carl Page wrote, 'We are entering a changing world. We shall take part in, or witness, developments in science, medicine, and industry that we cannot dream of today.'[4] Forty-one years later, on 15 September, 1997, his son registered Google, thereby

---

[3] Nicholas Carson, 'The Story of How Larry Page Got Forced from the Top of Google and Came Back a Decade Later', *Business Insider*, 25 April 2014. Available at https://www.businessinsider.com/larry-page-the-untold-story-2014-4; accessed on 15 March 2021.

[4] http://googlepress.blogspot.com/2009/05/larry-pages-university-of-michigan.html; accessed on 15 March 2021.

creating the biggest change in the technological world and revolutionizing the Internet for all mankind.

At the age of twelve, Larry had cried after reading the sad biography of the brilliant inventor Nikola Tesla, who died in debt and obscurity. It was also at the age of twelve that he knew that he would start a company someday, a company that would make a difference, one that would not merely invent world-changing technologies but also become accessible to the global population so that people could actually use them to change their lives.

Always taking things apart to find out how they were built and brimming with ideas about building new things, Larry had been dreaming up revolutionary schemes even as a child. Ever since his childhood, he had big, improbable dreams and did everything he could to make them a reality as quickly as possible. As an undergrad at the University of Michigan, he'd proposed something he called a PRT, or personal rapid transit system—a driverless monorail with separate cars for every rider that would help students commute between the central and north campus. One idea was about building a long rope that would run from the Earth's surface all the way into orbit, making it cheaper to put objects in space. Another proposal called for solar kites that would draw energy from space.

His ideas were always big and often seemed improbable to those around him until he went ahead and made them a reality. In college, he wanted to find out if really large images could be printed without spending too much money, so he built an inkjet printer using Legos! Larry really seems to have internalized a slogan he had heard at a leadership training programme at the University of Michigan—to have a 'healthy disregard for the impossible'. He mentioned this again in the speech he gave in 2009. 'Many things that people labor hard to do now, like cooking, cleaning, and driving will require much less human time in the future. That is, if we 'have a healthy disregard for the impossible' and actually build new solutions.'[5]

> *You can do almost anything*
> *if you have a disregard for the impossible.*

But Tesla's biography had also taught Page an invaluable lesson. It wasn't enough to think of big ideas; they had to be commercialized and made to reach the people. At a TED Talk in March 2014, 'Where's Google Going Next?', Page said, 'I think invention is not enough. If you invent something, Tesla invented electric power that we use, but he struggled to get it out to people. That had to be done by other people. It took a long time. And I think if we can actually combine both things, where we have an innovation and invention focus, plus the ability to really [sic]—a company that can really commercialize things and get them to people in a way that's positive for the world and to give people hope.'[6]

Google was incorporated on 4 September 1998—two years after Page's life-changing dream—from a friend's garage in Menlo Park. Larry and Sergei created a visually simple and user-friendly homepage using Larry's basic HTML knowledge since they didn't have a webpage developer. And since there was limited amount of physical space, Larry was constantly working to keep the servers efficient so they could fit more onto the computers in their warehouses. This made Google very fast. By 2000, it had indexed one billion URLs and had become the most comprehensive search engine of the time.

---

[5] http://googlepress.blogspot.com/2009/05/larry-pages-university-of-michigan.html; accessed on 15 March 2021.
[6] https://www.ted.com/talks/larry_page_where_s_google_going_next?language=en; accessed on 15 March 2021.

Larry's love for speed is reflected in all of Google's products. In 2004, Paul Buchheit brought Gmail to Larry's open cubicle office for a review. Paul had created Gmail and wanted to make sure everything was okay before its launch. As he pulled the programme up on Larry's computer, he noticed that Larry seemed a little disappointed. 'It's too slow,' Larry said. 'It was loading just fine,' Paul disagreed. No, Larry insisted. It had taken a full 600 milliseconds for the page to load. 'You can't know that,' Paul said. But when he looked up the server logs, he realized Larry was right. Gmail had taken exactly 600 milliseconds to load.[7] Larry attributes his love for high-speed computing to his musical background. He played the saxophone and learnt music composition as a child. In an interview with *Fortune* in 2014, he said, 'If you think about it from a music point of view, if you're a percussionist, you hit something, it's got to happen in milliseconds, fractions of a second.'[8]

As of 25 March 2021, searching for Larry Page on Google produces about 289,000,000 results in just a few seconds.

Early on in Google's life, Heather Cairns, the woman responsible for hiring Google's first 200 employees, spotted Larry talking intently with a janitor after work hours. When she later asked Larry what they were discussing, Larry said 'I want to know how everyone does their job.' He then went on to praise the janitor's method of placing empty trash bags at the bottom of each barrel so he could replace them easily. 'It's very efficient,' Larry said approvingly, 'and he saves time doing that, and I learned from that.'

---

[7] https://news.ycombinator.com/item?id=9138814; accessed on 15 March 2021.
[8] Miguel Helft, 'How Music Education Influenced Larry Page', *Fortune*, 18 November 2014. Available at https://fortune.com/2014/11/18/larry-page-music-education/; accessed on 15 March 2021.

Look for opportunities to learn.
There are lessons hidden everywhere.

Larry's love for efficiency and creativity has led him to create technology that overwhelmingly makes life better for humans and will only continue to do so. 'Anything you can imagine probably is doable,' Larry told Google investors in 2012. 'You just have to imagine it and work on it.'[9]

And that's what he does indeed! One day in 1998, when Cairns walked into the company's first office in the garage at Menlo Park, she caught Larry and Sergei playing with Legos. In front of them was a contraption with robot arms and rubber wheels at the end. On being asked what they were doing, Larry explained, 'We're trying to figure out how to turn a page of a book without a human hand. Someday we're going to put every publication in the world on the Internet so everybody has access to it.'[10]

Google Books launched in 2003 and has come to encompass more than 40 million titles!

Everything can become a reality,
if you simply use your imagination and work on it.

Not long after, in 1998, Larry drove around Palo Alto for an entire day with a small handheld camera. After driving for a few feet, he would stop and take a few pictures. On returning home, he uploaded the pictures to his computer. The exercise

---

[9]Nicholas Carson, 'The Story of How Larry Page Got Forced from the Top of Google and Came Back a Decade Later', *Business Insider*, 25 April 2014. Available at https://www.businessinsider.com/larry-page-the-untold-story-2014-4; accessed on 15 March 2021.

[10]Nicholas Carson, 'The Story of How Larry Page Got Forced from the Top of Google and Came Back a Decade Later', *Business Insider*, 25 April 2014. Available at https://www.businessinsider.com/larry-page-the-untold-story-2014-4; accessed on 15 March 2021.

convinced him of the feasibility of his latest big idea. Google could put cameras on cars and drive every street in the world, photographing all the way. The result would be an online digital, searchable representation of the entire physical world.

Google Street launched in 2007, and by 2014, every thoroughfare in 50 countries was made viewable from almost every web browser on the planet!

By 2005, Larry envisioned putting handheld computers with access to Google in every person's pocket. The same year, Google acquired the start-up Android!

Taking up ambitious challenges and envisioning new ideas that can change the world is what keeps Larry going. At a product meeting of Google, he is famously known to have said, 'We build products that leverage technology to solve huge problems for hundreds of millions of people. Look at Android. Look at Gmail. Look at Google Maps. Look at Google Search. That's what we do. We build products you can't live without.'[11]

Technology, he believes, can help solve a number of world problems. In his 2009 speech at the University of Michigan, he told the graduates about how he and his wife had once visited a village in India where sewage ran in the streets. The sewage was infected with polio—the same disease that had killed his father. 'He would have been very upset that polio still persists, even though we have a vaccine,' Larry said. 'The world is on the verge of eliminating polio, with 328 people infected so far this year. Let's get it done soon.'[12]

---

[11]Nicholas Carson, 'The Story of How Larry Page Got Forced from the Top of Google and Came Back a Decade Later', *Business Insider*, 25 April 2014. Available at https://www.businessinsider.com/larry-page-the-untold-story-2014-4; accessed on 15 March 2021.

[12]Nicholas Carson, 'The Story of How Larry Page Got Forced from the Top of Google and Came Back a Decade Later', *Business Insider*, 25 April 2014. Available

Most of his technological visions for making the world a better place is now worked upon at Google's parent company Alphabet Inc., established in 2015 and of which Larry was the CEO till December 2019. In 2010, Google established Google X, now a subsidiary of Alphabet Inc. Through Google X, or just X Development LLC, Larry is able to give many of his visionary, almost-sci-fi ideas wings. It calls these ideas 'moonshots'. A moonshot is defined by the company as 'the intersection of a big problem, a radical solution and breakthrough technology'.[13] There are many more of them, from hot-air balloons that broadcast the Internet spectrum, providing access to areas of the world that have lacked it, to Android-powered watches to self-driven cars and even artificial brains.

The overriding objective behind all of Larry's larger-than-life ideas is envisioning a world where everything is connected with and understood by an artificially intelligent computer that can perceive the patterns in our activities and anticipate our needs before we even know we have them. Having stepped away from Google, Larry's focus is now on research on transhumanism.

What seems crazy to the world today clearly becomes credible tomorrow through the unlimited means Larry has at hand and with his passion for making the impossible possible. His motto is: 'If you're not doing some things that are crazy, then you're doing the wrong things.'[14]

Every idea worth pursuing should at first seem a little crazy.

---

at https://www.businessinsider.com/larry-page-the-untold-story-2014-4; accessed on 15 March 2021.

[13]*Hubxygen*, 'Insights from X, the Moonshot Factory', 17 November 2020. Available at https://www.hubxygen.com/post/x-the-moonshot-factory; accessed on 15 March 2021.

[14]Steven Levy, 'Google's Larry Page on Why Moon Shots Matter', *Wired*, 17 January 2013. Available at https://www.wired.com/2013/01/ff-qa-larry-page/; accessed on 15 March 2021.

Chapter 11

HUSTLING FOR HAPPINESS

*Lilly Singh: YouTuber, Author,
Host of* A Little Late with Lilly Singh

'Hello my name is Lilly, and I ain't a white man/ My skin's got some colour and it ain't a spray tan,' rapped Lilly Singh in the first segment of the premiere of her talk show.[1] With the rap, Lilly addressed and defied stereotypes of race, colour, ethnicity and gender. At 30, Lilly has created history by being the first queer woman of Indian descent to have her own late night show, *A Little Late with Lilly Singh*, on NBC.

In a world where race, colour, ethnicity, gender and sexuality are obstacles for people, Lilly sees them as superpowers. Taking on the moniker of 'Superwoman' for herself, Lilly works towards the goal of 'One Love'—a universal love and respect expressed by all people for all people, a feat no less than a superhero task in a world that is so divided. A seemingly ordinary Canadian woman, Lilly has been breaking stereotypes and promoting inclusion, acceptance and tolerance with her extraordinarily positive personality ever since she first started as a YouTuber in 2010.

Lilly says that her story is essentially 'a story of happiness,

---

[1]https://www.youtube.com/watch?v=NppK_T_J8qc; accessed on 15 March 2021.

of a sad person deciding to be happy and sharing that message with the world.[2] She began making YouTube videos as a way to combat depression. Making herself and other people laugh through her observational and sketch-comedy videos became a form of therapy for her. In an interview with *Buzzfeed*, she said, 'I was coming out of a really difficult time period and I wanted a way to cheer myself up and also cheer other people up. And from a business point of view, when I discovered YouTube, I saw that there were no South Asian females doing it, so I thought it was a great opportunity.'[3]

Follow your heart.

Lilly's first YouTube video was a piece of spoken poetry on religion. At the time, she was volunteering at the local Gurudwara in Scarborough. The video only garnered 70 views and is nothing like the videos she has become known for. Soon after graduating with a degree in Psychology from York University, Lilly's parents expected her to pursue a master's degree. But a linear career path did not appeal to Lilly. The lack of interest and enthusiasm in her future prospects led her down a path of deep depression where she was unable to even get out of bed for days. Upset at herself for being confused about her future, angry at herself for wasting the money her parents had invested in her education made her further go on a downward spiral.

---

[2] Julia Felsenthal, 'YouTube Star Lilly Singh (aka Superwoman) on Her New Documentary', *Vogue*, 11 February 2016. Available at https://www.vogue.com/article/lilly-singh-superwoman-profile; accessed on 15 March 2021.

[3] PJ, 'Uncut Interview With Lilly Singh (aka YouTube Star IISuperwomanII)', *BuzzFeed*, 1 February 2015. Available at https://www.buzzfeed.com/prajakta/uncut-interview-with-lilly-singh-aka-youtube-sta-184om?utm_term=.agAwpJRA4#.pnB9yR0v1; accessed on 15 March 2021.

Aimless and unhappy, one day Lilly stumbled upon a video by a 24-year-old New Yorker Jenna Marbles. Marbles's videos attracted a huge audience because of her personality. It made Lilly realize the possibilities of YouTube. The very next day, she made her first video. Her videos initially catered to second-generation South Asian millennials living in the West, for whom the videos became even more relatable when Lilly acted out slightly caricatured and fictionalized versions of her parents. In her gap year, still working at the collection agency where she had taken up a job that she had started detesting, the YouTube videos became Lilly's passion. Using the platform not just for self-expression but also for self-improvement, she learned from other videos about lighting, camera equipment, graphics and sound effects. Within six months, she hit a thousand subscribers.

Often seen wearing a T-shirt that says 'Hustle Hard', Lilly believes in the power of relentless hustling. To her, hustling means working hard and smart every single day because she loves what she does and it gives her immense joy. In one of her videos with her entire family, when asked for the one word they can use to describe her, her sister, Tina, who incidentally has her own YouTube channel now, immediately says, 'hardworking'. In an interview with *Vogue*, Lilly says, 'When I was younger, I had this fairy tale that you can have eight hours of sleep and be a healthy, balanced, person and still achieve your goals. That hasn't always been the case. On an average day, I will spend 90% of my waking moments working on Superwoman. I'm a huge workaholic. My hobby *is* Superwoman.'[4]

---

[4] Julia Felsenthal, 'YouTube Star Lilly Singh (aka Superwoman) on Her New Documentary', *Vogue*, 11 February 2016. Available at https://www.vogue.com/article/lilly-singh-superwoman-profile; accessed on 15 March 2021.

Work hard. Hustle hard.

Lilly had no idea that creating content for YouTube could become a career. That changed when she met fellow YouTuber Allen Buckle in 2011. They met in Buckle's house which, he told her, he had bought with money from making videos on YouTube. 'I was blown away,' Lilly recalls. 'I had no idea people could make a living posting videos.'[5] When Lilly told her parents that she wanted to become a YouTube star instead of going to grad school, her father gave her one year to focus on YouTube. The deal was if she couldn't make a career out of it in a year, she would have to go back to school. Her first invoice from YouTube was only about $18. But by the time she hit the one-year mark, she had 100,000 subscribers. Within two years, she had a million subscribers.

For Lilly, though, being a YouTuber was not merely about having a new career or making money. And even though with 100-odd videos a year, she was making about $2.5 million, her driving force was the chance to influence and inspire other young people with positivity and help strengthen their mental health. By the time she had three million subscribers in 2014, her uniquely personal brand had already gone beyond her control. Her fans call themselves Team Super or Unicorns—Lilly is obsessed with the mythical creature—and cheer for her, send her messages of love, write fanfiction about her, devote Instagram accounts to her and make YouTube videos about her videos. She soon signed a manager, Sarah Weichsel, and grew her team. In an interview with *Toronto Life*, Weichsel said that the first thing Lilly said

---

[5]Emily Landau, 'Lilly Singh Goes to Hollywood', *Toronto Life*, 21 March 2017. Available at https://torontolife.com/city/life/inside-dizzying-world-lilly-singh-torontos-accidental-megastar/; accessed on 15 March 2021.

to her when they met was 'I want world domination.'[6]

World domination was not a far-flung goal for her. When Lilly set out on a 31-day world tour of 27 cities in countries like India, Australia, Dubai, Singapore, the UK and the US in 2016, she realized just how much people loved her. The tour was a mix of singing, rapping, dancing, comedy and motivational speeches. She released a documentary about it and called it *A Trip to Unicorn Island*. In the interview with *Vogue*, she said, '*Unicorn Island* is the synonym for my happy place. It's a really beautiful message: that happiness is one of the hardest things you'll ever fight for, but it's the only thing worth fighting for.'[7] Even with her show, Lilly sends out messages of positivity. In an interview with *Marie Claire*, she said, 'When you watch my show, you will feel happiness. You turn on a little Lilly Singh, it's going to be good times.'[8]

Fight for happiness.

Born to Malwinder Kaur and Sukhwinder Singh, who immigrated to Canada from Punjab, India, on 26 September 1988, Lilly and her older sister, Tina, were raised in Scarborough, Toronto, and brought up in a multicultural environment. Lilly learnt the art of hard work and hustling from her parents. Her father, Sukhwinder, after coming to Canada in 1972, found jobs as a factory worker, cab driver and furniture salesman, finally earning enough money for his

---

[6]Emily Landau, 'Lilly Singh Goes to Hollywood', *Toronto Life*, 21 March 2017. Available at https://torontolife.com/city/life/inside-dizzying-world-lilly-singh-torontos-accidental-megastar/; accessed on 15 March 2021.

[7]Julia Felsenthal, 'YouTube Star Lilly Singh (aka Superwoman) on Her New Documentary', *Vogue*, 11 February 2016. Available at https://www.vogue.com/article/lilly-singh-superwoman-profile; accessed on 15 March 2021.

[8]Allison Glock, 'It's Lilly Singh's Turn to Ask the Questions', *Marie Claire*, 11 September 2019. Available at https://www.marieclaire.com/celebrity/a28944411/lilly-singh-interview-2019/; accessed on 15 March 2021.

wife to immigrate in 1981. Her mother, Malwinder, worked at a company that produced CDs and cassettes. Eventually, Sukhwinder acquired leases for 11 gas stations, and, by the early '80s, they bought a home in Malvern. Lilly herself has hustled in many jobs as a collection agent, drive-thru cashier at a Canadian fast-food chain Harvey's, camera saleswoman and dance instructor, till she found her passion and calling.

Lilly's parents are extremely supportive of her career choice and have appeared in a number of her videos. Their daughter's love for music, dance, acting and entertainment was not unknown to them. Even when Lilly was eight, she would carry around camcorders and record her daily life and often act out skits in front of the camera. The passion and obsession led her to become the highest earning female creator on YouTube in 2016. She was featured on *Forbes*'s top influencers in entertainment list in 2017.

That very year, Lilly released her inspirational book, *How to Be a Bawse: A Guide to Conquering Life* and became a *New York Times* bestselling author. The book motivated thousands of young people to believe in and love themselves. The book is Lilly's guide to living in this world and making it a better place through positivity and self-love. Some of the chapters are titled: 'Schedule Inspiration', 'Be Unapologetically Yourself' and 'Be Nice to People.' In an interview with *Elle Canada*, Lilly said that being a 'bawse' is all about taking charge of your life so you can achieve your goals. A bawse is not restricted to the workplace, she said. 'It's like a lifestyle. It's your personal life, how you communicate, how you hustle.'[9] To *Marie Claire*,

---

[9]Liz Guber, 'It Took Lilly Singh a While to Realize She was Funny', *Elle Canada*, 11 April 2017. Available at https://www.ellecanada.com/culture/celebrity/it-took-lilly-singh-a-while-to-realize-she-was-funny; accessed on 15 March 2021.

she had said, '"Bawse" is "like a boss", but so epic I had to change the spelling. It's someone who exudes confidence, turns heads, gets hurt efficiently, communicates effectively and hustles relentlessly.'[10]

Be a 'Bawse'

Today, Lilly's YouTube channel has close to 15 million subscribers. A number of her videos are collaborations with celebrities from across the world. Dwayne 'The Rock' Johnson tops the list. Lilly admits that she had been obsessed with him ever since she was in third grade. 'If they ever announced my name over the PA system at school, they'd call me Lilly "The Rock" Singh,' she says.[11] Today, these very celebrities are her friends and all help in promoting her message of positivity and support the idea of being true to yourself that Lilly vociferously stands for.

A bundle of energy, Lilly begins almost all of her videos animatedly with 'Whaddup! It's your girrrrrrrrrl Superwoman!' But just like she exudes confidence in front of her millions of subscribers, she is also not afraid to admit when she is unhappy and not feeling quite up to it. In 2018, she decided to take a break from YouTube for a while, telling her followers: 'I want to be honest with you, I could be happier. I'm not my optimal happiness right now, I could be mentally healthier. I don't feel like I'm completely mentally healthy. There's a lot going on up here that I need to address and I'm not able to

---

[10]Allison Glock, 'It's Lilly Singh's Turn to Ask the Questions', *Marie Claire*, 11 September 2019. Available at https://www.marieclaire.com/celebrity/a28944411/lilly-singh-interview-2019/; accessed on 15 March 2021.

[11]Emily Landau, 'Lilly Singh Goes to Hollywood', *Toronto Life*, 21 March 2017. Available at https://torontolife.com/city/life/inside-dizzying-world-lilly-singh-torontos-accidental-megastar/; accessed on 15 March 2021.

constantly pumping out content [sic].'[12] Her refreshing honesty is what endears her to her loyal fans and her normalcy makes her more accessible to them. If Lilly can do it, if she can overcome her obstacles and become happy, if she can follow her heart and be successful, so can they.

Besides being a role model for young people around the world, Lilly is also a goodwill UNICEF ambassador, the first digital personality to be so. In one of her videos, she is seen collaborating with Michelle Obama to discuss her philanthropic campaign, #GirlLove, in order to inspire positivity and support among young girls and women and eradicate girl-on-girl bullying. With the support of other influencers, she helps promote the education of girls with profits from the sale of Rafiki bracelets made by mothers in Kenya. Lilly travelled to Kenya where she met with the women who make the bracelets which she helped design and even the children whose education is supported by the bracelet's profits. She also created a bracelet for the men who participated in the #GirlLove campaign. UNICEF Deputy Executive Director Justin Forsyth said about her, 'Lilly Singh is already a Superwoman, helping empower girls around the world—and we are delighted that she will lend her passion and her powerful voice to speak up on behalf of the most vulnerable children.'[13]

Lilly is not one to pause. In 2015, Lilly moved from the suburbs of Toronto to Los Angeles. Season 2 of *A Little Late with Lilly Singh* was launched in May 2020, for which she shot most of the episodes from a home setup due to the pandemic.

---

[12]https://www.youtube.com/watch?time_continue=3&v=-5OfFk5c01o&feature=emb_logo; accessed on 15 March 2021.

[13]https://www.unicef.org/media/media_96640.html; accessed on 15 March 2021.

Lilly also has a new show called a *Sketchy Time with Lilly Singh*, which features sketches about the challenging chaos of 2020 and helps bring people joy through comedy. Lilly is the executive producer of both shows under her company Unicorn Island Productions, which she set up in 2018. She will be voicing Penny in *Riverdance: The Animated Adventure* and Pickles in *HitPig*. Lilly will also be partnering with children's media company PocketWatch to create her own animated musical short film titled *Lilly Singh's Proud Princess*, where she will voice a young girl that goes on a journey to discover her identity and pride. All her endeavours and projects are ways in which she promotes self-love and overcoming fear.

In her *Marie Claire* interview, Lilly says, 'Loving myself was a very hard lesson. I want to love myself, but I also want to be myself.'[14] She is mastering the art gradually and publicly so that others who face a similar struggle can be inspired by her journey. In a world where artifice, divisiveness, judgement and hatred thrive, Lilly reminds everyone about the power that lies in being oneself, being natural, honest, open and fearless. Step into her website and you will find the line: 'I thoroughly believe in crying, yelling, pulling my hair out, and experiencing heartache, BUT once I'm done I dissect the pain and learn lessons from it.'[15] It's what makes her Lilly Singh, it's what makes her Bawse, it's what makes her a Superwoman!

Be yourself. Love yourself.

---

[14] Allison Glock, 'It's Lilly Singh's Turn to Ask the Questions', *Marie Claire*, 11 September 2019. Available at https://www.marieclaire.com/celebrity/a28944411/lilly-singh-interview-2019/; accessed on 15 March 2021.

[15] https://lillysingh.com/pages/about-lilly-singh; accessed on 15 March 2021.

Chapter 12

CONNECTING THE WORLD

Mark Zuckerberg: Co-founder of Facebook

In one of his earliest interviews in 2004, Mark Zuckerberg said to *CNBC* that when 'thefacebook.com' was first launched on 4 February that year, they were hoping for about 400 to 500 people to sign up. But by December of that year, it had already reached a million users. The aim was initially to have most of the colleges and universities subscribe to it and make it interesting enough for people to want to keep coming back. One of the things it made possible was for people to find 'some interesting information' about other people. By 2020, Zuckerberg's revolution, now known simply as Facebook, has made it possible for over 2.74 billion active users to do much more than just find interesting information about each other.

A video taken by Edward Zuckerberg[1] captures the now historic moment a young Mark reads out his acceptance email from Harvard. Zuckerberg posted the video on his own Facebook page—a portal he actively uses to share snippets and highlights from his life with his network of friends and followers.

In Harvard, Mark became known as the go-to computer

---

[1] https://www.youtube.com/watch?v=gsefnhTK5lc; accessed on 15 March 2021.

programmer and, by his sophomore year, he had already built two programmes: CourseMatch and FaceMash. CourseMatch could let the students see what courses their classmates were enrolled in at Harvard, so that they could make a choice before each semester. FaceMash was like a precursor to Facebook. It was created just for fun; it presented the user with two pictures of either male or female students at Harvard and asked them to choose the better-looking one. Although both programmes became extremely popular among the students, the university shut down the latter after it was deemed inappropriate. Soon after, Zuckerberg's interest in coding and building things led him to create a website through which the students of Harvard could find out more about their fellow classmates. Harvard already had existing Face Books: books with the names and pictures of all those who lived in the student dorms. A part of Facebook's inspiration may have also been a photo address book at the Phillips Exeter Academy, the prep school that Zuckerberg attended. The photo directory listed students' names, photos, their friends and their phone numbers. Zuckerberg's brainchild offered something more—a portal that gave students access to not only each other's personal information but also their personality, their likes and dislikes. He transformed his idea into reality with the help of his friends and classmates Eduardo Saverin, Andrew McCollum, Dustin Moskovitz and Chris Hughes, and launched 'thefacebook. com' from his dorm room in Kirkland House on the Harvard campus.

With Facebook's business idea taking off, Zuckerberg decided to drop out of Harvard and move to Paolo Alto in June 2004 to concentrate on his creation which had now dropped 'the' and '.com' from its name and was known only as Facebook. The first investment that Facebook received was a sum of $500,000 from one of the founders of PayPal, Peter Thiel. By then, its popularity and success had spread to other schools and by 2005, it had nearly five million users across 15 campuses. In 2006, Facebook was expanded from college students and high schoolers to anyone who was over 13 and had a valid email address. Even then, in an early interview in 2005, Zuckerberg said that he would go back to Harvard if the business venture fell through. Twelve years later, during Harvard's three hundred and sixty-sixth graduation ceremony, when invited to give the commencement speech, Zuckerberg said, 'If I get through this speech, it'll be the first time I actually finish something at Harvard.'[2] But he finished just more than his speech. He finally received an honorary Doctor of Laws degree.

At the same commencement speech, he mentioned that the best part of going to Harvard was the chance to meet awesome people. At his first class, Computer Science 12, the young Mark threw on a T-shirt inside out and backwards with the tag sticking out the front. Only one guy spoke to him in class that day—K.X. Jin. They ended up working on their problem sets together, and now Jin is the head of health at Facebook.

Don't be afraid to take the road less travelled.

Born into an educated family on 14 May 1984 to Edward Zuckerberg, a dentist, and Karen Zuckerberg, a psychiatrist, Mark grew up in Dobbs Ferry, New York. The second of four children, Mark has three sisters: Arielle, Randi and Donna. Edward taught his son Atari BASIC programming in the

---

[2]https://news.harvard.edu/gazette/story/2017/05/mark-zuckerbergs-speech-as-written-for-harvards-class-of-2017/; accessed on 15 March 2021.

1990s. After observing the young Mark's interest and talent in computer programming, his parents hired software developer David Newman to tutor him privately. At home, the young Zuckerberg built a software programme called 'ZuckNet' that allowed all the computers between the house and his father's dental office to communicate with each other—a primitive version of AOL's Instant Messenger that was launched the following year. He also enjoyed developing games and communication tools just for fun. Seeing his potential, Edward enrolled him into a graduate course in software programming at Mercy College while he was still in high school.

But Zuckerberg is unlike the stereotypical geek. His interests are varied and so are his talents. His Facebook likes include Rihanna, Linkin Park, Shakira, Lady Gaga and TV shows such as *Game of Thrones* and *The West Wing*. At Exeter, he was captain of the fencing team and received a diploma in Classics. His obsession with the Classics is famous among those who know him. He loves *The Aeneid* so much that his colleagues at Facebook have even found him quoting from it at team meetings. He also enjoys his pranks. One of his most memorable ones so far, the prank website, FaceMash, also led him to meet yet another 'awesome' person at Harvard— his future wife, Priscilla. Expecting that he was going to be thrown out of Harvard, Zuckerberg's friends threw him a farewell party. Priscilla was at that party. The young Mark and Priscilla met while waiting in line for the restroom in the Pfoho Belltower. The romantic line that won her over was, 'I'm going to get kicked out in three days, so we need to go on a date quickly.'[3] On 19 May 2012, they got married.

---

[3] https://news.harvard.edu/gazette/story/2017/05/mark-zuckerbergs-speech-as-written-for-harvards-class-of-2017/; accessed on 15 March 2021.

But Zuckerberg's sophomoric self, he admits, has changed in most other ways, from an excited teenager who had built a website whose goal was simply to find out a bunch of information about someone when their name was typed into a tech tycoon whose goal, according to his own Facebook page, is 'bringing the world closer together'. In the bio section of his page, Zuckerberg writes simply, 'I'm trying to make the world a more open place.'[4]

*Even if your goals change,
don't give up on what you have started.*

As early as 2005, Zuckerberg started thinking of how Facebook could become a resource for connecting people, for finding old friends from middle school or high school, perhaps. Finding long-lost friends and connecting people is definitely why Facebook is so popular. Separated as children in 1954 when their parents divorced, Allan Healy and Margaret Mitchell found each other on Facebook after living most of their lives about 800 km apart without any contact. In another instance, the chief executive of the Bermuda Heart Foundation took to Facebook to share the inspiring story of one Simone Barton. Simone needed a kidney transplant and though several donors had volunteered, none were a match. With just one 'status' shared with her 162 friends, she was able to find an old colleague who was the perfect compatible match for Simone. The transplant was a success. On 2 February, a Michigan mom started a Facebook page to solicit birthday wishes to cheer up her disabled son, Colin, who said he didn't want an eleventh birthday party because he thought he didn't have friends. According to an article in *TIME Magazine*, about a

---

[4]https://www.facebook.com/zuck; accessed on 15 March 2021.

week and a half later, he had 60,000 of them on Facebook. Now the 'Colin's Friends' page has more than 1.6 million likes. Zuckerberg himself shared a heart-warming story on his page. In the 1960s, a woman named Muriel was asked by her church in New York if she would look after three young boys after their mother passed away. They stayed with the family for over a year but later lost touch. Nearly 50 years later, Muriel asked her daughter Joanne to help find the boys. Using Facebook, Joanne made contact with one of the boys in less than an hour. Muriel travelled to Mexico to meet with him. She's now reunited on Facebook with all three of them.

As a father of two girls, Maxima and August, Zuckerberg is most concerned about whether they will be proud of the work that he is doing. He is willing to face any challenges and, in an interview with *CNN* in 2018, he said that he is grateful that he gets to work on some of the most important problems in the world today. At the Harvard commencement speech, he said, 'The challenge for our generation is creating a world where everyone has a sense of purpose.' He even explains how this can be done: 'By taking on big meaningful projects together, by redefining equality so everyone has the freedom to pursue purpose, and by building community across the world.'[5] Facebook is that community that makes it possible for Zuckerberg to create the greatest possible impact in the world.

Find your sense of purpose.

For someone who became a millionaire at the age of 22 and a billionaire by 23, Zuckerberg is known to be quite frugal and not too concerned about money. Viacom contemplated

---

[5] https://news.harvard.edu/gazette/story/2017/05/mark-zuckerbergs-speech-as-written-for-harvards-class-of-2017/; accessed on 15 March 2021.

buying Facebook for $75 million in March 2005. That same year, Yahoo! and Microsoft offered much more. Zuckerberg turned them all down. (It was later, in 2007, that Microsoft acquired 1.6 per cent equity stake in Facebook.)

For his senior project at Exeter, along with a friend, Zuckerberg had created a software programme called Synapse. Synapse used machine learning to determine a user's music listening habits and recommended more music based on the genre, artist and taste. When news of the software's existence spread, AOL and Microsoft expressed their interest to buy Synapse and recruit Zuckerberg. He had turned them down then too.

Even though today he has a beautiful home that is powered by an AI butler, in an interview in 2010, he said that he found all of his apartments on Craigslist.

Seemingly indifferent to money, Zuckerberg still is a great strategist. He knows that his goal of creating the greatest possible impact in the world would be realized only when Facebook becomes accessible to everyone and more and more people find it useful. Even as early as 2005, he was thinking about enhancing the user experience with the data that the users were providing to the site and targeting stuff towards them in a way that was unprecedented. Today, much of Facebook's revenues come from targeted contextual advertising. The number of users and the time they spend on the site is converted into advertising revenues. This has been a heavily criticized feature of Facebook as users feel that their privacy is being constantly invaded. Most of the remaining revenue comes from deductions from any purchase made through the Facebook payment system.

As part of his endeavour to give the users the best experience, Zuckerberg makes acquisitions that continue their operation as independent entities under Facebook's umbrella. Some of the popular ones are the mobile photo-sharing app Instagram developed by Mike Krieger and Kevin Systrom, acquired in April 2012 for $1 billion in cash and stock, and the instant messaging application WhatsApp, founded by Jan Koum and Brian Acton acquired for $22 billion in October 2014.

Create something that is useful to the customer.

Even though Zuckerberg has been taking one giant leap at a time, by his own admission, he is very awkward in public. He is a shy and private person. He rarely speaks to the media and doesn't quite enjoy making public appearances, an occupational hazard for him. His calm demeanour stands him in good stead through all the highs and lows that his company faces. Facebook has seen its share of lows and Zuckerberg himself has been criticized for issues such as user privacy, the way in which news is reported and distributed on Facebook and the negative psychological effects that Facebook can have on its users, among many others. Facebook has faced several litigation cases over the years and a number of governments have even chosen to ban the site in their countries. Most recently, during the US elections, Facebook was accused of instigating violence through the spread of political misinformation. Zuckerberg says that he wants to reduce the amount of politics on the site and is constantly trying to create a balance between free expression, safety and privacy and social equity on his platform.[6] And the truth is,

---

[6] Audrey Conklin, 'Zuckerberg Says Facebook Wants to "Reduce the Amount of Politics" on Platform', *Fox Business*, 2 February 2021. Available at https://www.foxbusiness.com/technology/zuckerberg-facebook-reduce-politics; accessed on 15 March 2021.

as proven by the user numbers, the world still can't seem to do without Facebook. During the pandemic, the site was used as a go-to communications tool for most people.

Like most of Facebook's users, what Zuckerberg does when he wakes up first thing in the morning is check Facebook. That's how he gets updated on what's going on in the world, he says.[7] He doesn't believe in spending time on taking decisions on small things. That is mostly the reason why his standard attire is often just a grey T-shirt, blue jeans and sneakers but also because colours don't matter to him much. An online test he had taken made him realize that he has red–green colour blindness. Perhaps one of the reasons why blue is Facebook's dominant colour. Zuckerberg admitted in an interview with the *New Yorker*, 'Blue is the richest color for me—I can see all of blue.'[8]

In his commencement speech at Harvard, Zuckerberg said, 'Let's give everyone the freedom to pursue their purpose— not only because it's the right thing to do, but because when more people can turn their dreams into something great, we're all better for it.'[9] After the birth of their daughter Maxima, Zuckerberg and his wife wrote a letter to her: 'Max, we love you and feel a great responsibility to leave the world a better place for you and all children.'[10] Through the Chan Zuckerberg Initiative, the couple pledged to donate 99 per cent of their

---

[7] https://youtu.be/aNYLXmlPVTw; accessed on 15 March 2021.
[8] Jose Antonio Vargas, 'The Face of Facebook', *The New Yorker*, 20 September 2010. Available at https://www.newyorker.com/magazine/2010/09/20/the-face-of-facebook; accessed on 15 March 2021.
[9] https://news.harvard.edu/gazette/story/2017/05/mark-zuckerbergs-speech-as-written-for-harvards-class-of-2017/; accessed on 15 March 2021.
[10] Mark Zuckerberg (@zuck), 'A Letter to Our Daughter', *Facebook*. Available at https://www.facebook.com/notes/mark-zuckerberg/a-letter-to-our-daughter/10153375081581634/; accessed on 15 March 2021.

Facebook shares—worth about $45 billion—within their lifetime to promote human potential, equality and world development. As part of his goal to 'create the greatest possible impact on the world',[11] Zuckerberg contributes regularly to social causes and organizations such as the Newark Public Schools and San Francisco General Hospital. He contributed $25 million to help victims of Ebola in West Africa. He also meets with leaders from other countries in an effort to shape future generations and work out solutions to help tackle various global social problems.

Sheryl Sandberg, the COO of Facebook, once recounted a story of how, for a party, Zuckerberg wanted to make marshmallows. Immediately, Sandberg admits, she was certain that the marshmallows would be perfect. The reason: Zuckerberg had the perseverance and the patience required to make perfect marshmallows.[12] This persistence and relentless striving is what made Zuckerberg create in Facebook one of the most powerful technologies ever built to increase connection between people separated by borders of nation, language, religion and culture.

Create an impact on the world.

---

[11] Mark Zuckerberg (@zuck), 'Building Global Community', *Facebook*. Available at https://www.facebook.com/notes/mark-zuckerberg/building-global-community/10154544292806634; accessed on 15 March 2021.

[12] Lisa Eadicicco, 'This Story about Marshmallows Explains How Mark Zuckerberg Gets Stuff Done', *TIME*, 16 November 2015. Available at https://time.com/4114354/mark-zuckerberg-success-tips-sheryl-sandberg/; accessed on 15 March 2021.

Chapter 13

INNOVATING TECHNOLOGY

Patrick Collison: Co-founder of Stripe

On Patrick Collison's website is a section titled, 'Advice for those between 10–20', and it is, he admits, advice that he would give to his younger self. The last advice on the list is: 'People who did great things often did so at very surprisingly young ages. (They were grayhaired when they became famous ... not when they did the work.) So, hurry up! You can do great things.'[1]

By 22, Patrick had already done some great things! And in his case, he was already famous by then.

Patrick and his brother John turned seven lines of code to build a software programme that organizations could connect to their apps and websites to instantly link it with credit cards and banking systems and receive payments, thereby facilitating and making online payments easier. All that the brothers wanted to really do was find a solution to a difficulty they were experiencing—a problem in implementing a method by which developers could accept online payment for their goods and services. Initially, they called themselves '/dev/payments' and almost ended up calling themselves 'paydaemon'. Later, they chose 'Stripe' out of a list of words, simply because they

---

[1] https://patrickcollison.com/advice; accessed on 15 March 2021.

thought it was a nice word and because it did not have any prior brand associations.

Both Patrick and John had been entrepreneurs from a very young age. When Patrick was just six months into MIT, the brothers were sitting in a pub when an idea came to them for an auction management system for online sellers. They initially called it 'Shuppa' (a play on the Irish word 'siopa', meaning 'shop'). Later, when they did not find funding for the company in their home country of Ireland, they moved to Silicon Valley, where they got together with two Oxford graduates and rebranded the company as Auctomatic, Inc. The company then went through Y Combinator and was bought by the Canadian company Live Current Media for $5 million in March 2008, making the brothers overnight millionaires.

Don't waste time.
You can do great things when you are young.

Just about a year later of having already turned into millionaires, one night in October 2009, while walking home after dinner, a discussion ensued between the brothers about the lack of financial infrastructure available online to make payments. The brothers felt sure that there was a need for an organization like it in the world. Even though the world has progressed with technology and smart phones, the business side of things still seemed like they were stuck in the archaic age. The brothers had even googled different permutations and combinations of keywords and phrases in order to find something like it but had eventually resigned to the fact that it just didn't exist. Realizing the gap in the market, John said to Patrick, 'Why don't we do it? It's probably not going to be all that hard', he added.

And so, Stripe was founded. Patrick was then only 21.

Born to Lily and Denis Collison on 9 September 1988 in County Tipperary, Ireland, entrepreneurship was built into Patrick's DNA. Denis ran a lakeside hotel and Lily started a corporate training company. Patrick said, in an interview with *The Independent*, '"Entrepreneur" is a long, fancy French word, but it didn't seem like something you aspire to. It seemed normal, because whatever your parents do seems normal.'[2]

Living in the Irish countryside, the three children—Patrick, John and Tommy—would have to find ways of keeping themselves entertained and busy. Patrick's daily routine often involved coming home from school, Gaelscoil Aonach Urmhumhan, Nenagh—about 40 minutes away from where they lived—walking to the library, getting home two new books and reading those books. It was just happenstance that one day Patrick brought home a programming book from the library and found it to be awesome. Patrick took his first computer course when he was only eight years old at the University of Limerick and began learning computer programming at the age of 10. At 16, he won the forty-first Young Scientist of the Year prize for his work with programming language, Lisp, and left school a year early to study Math at MIT—he took his place there based on a SAT score he received when he was 13.

As children, Patrick and John, close in age, often ended up spending a lot of time with each other. Always encouraged by their parents who inculcated in them an exploratory attitude, both brothers eventually created their own amateur websites and even hacked each other's websites to improve them.

---

[2] Ashlee Vance, 'How Ireland's Collison Brothers Turned Seven Lines of Code into a €9.2bn Tech Startup', *Independent.ie*, 3 August 2017. Available at https://www.independent.ie/business/technology/how-irelands-collison-brothers-turned-seven-lines-of-code-into-a-92bn-tech-startup-35993656.html; accessed on 15 March 2021.

Patrick jokes in an interview that it was because he took his duties as an older brother who had to protect the security of the slightly younger brother very seriously. The brothers also often competed with each other in coding to master the craft. Tommy, the youngest Collison sibling, has cerebral palsy. But there was never any wallowing in self-pity in the Collison household. Tommy has his own technological achievements to be proud of and is also a trained pilot like Patrick. In an interview, Patrick admits that the way his parents and his youngest brother approached the illness is what inspires him with his everyday challenges at Stripe.

> *Don't live in self-pity. You can achieve whatever you want despite all obstacles.*

Stripe faced its fair share of challenges in the beginning. Initially, it even seemed like a bad idea. In fact, Patrick claims that he still wakes up to a score of emails in his inbox telling him all the things Stripe is doing wrong. At the beginning, every argument seemed to go against the brothers, one of the most vital being the fact that they were two young Irish boys trying to set up a company in the US. During the first days of Stripe, Patrick and John spent all of their time programming. For months, they explored it, showed it to friends and saw how people interacted with it, programming and reprogramming along the way. The need for the company felt so compelling that to set it up Patrick even dropped out of MIT. Within two weeks of building their prototype, the first transaction occurred with a Y Combinator company called 280 North, whose founder, Ross Boucher, later joined Stripe as one of its first employees.

> *When you feel certain about an idea, you must work on it.*

The brothers realized that with Stripe, they had found a solution to a problem faced by most of the larger companies in the world. Their website says, 'Stripe is a technology company that builds economic infrastructure for the internet. Businesses of every size—from new startups to public companies—use our software to accept payments and manage their businesses online.'[3] Today, Stripe is available for business in over 43 countries with an impressive customer list that includes Google, Facebook, Microsoft, Amazon and Uber, among others. At the beginning, people got to know about Stripe through word of mouth. Friends of the team told other friends and so on. Today, Stripe counts Tesla's Elon Musk and PayPal founder Peter Thiel as investors. The company has benefited during the pandemic with more shoppers turning to e-commerce. A recent funding round suggests that investors are valuing Stripe at over $115 billion. Patrick and John keep the company policy simple: users first.

A quote by Greg LeMond, a professional cyclist who has won two world championships and three Tours de France, has stayed on with Patrick. 'It never gets easier—you just get faster.'[4] To Patrick, a cyclist himself, the saying rings true especially when faced with the everyday challenges of a start-up that is so young. One day, in the first two months in Stripe's journey, there had been a server outage due to a network failure. To Patrick, it had seemed disempowering and frustrating. However, it wasn't the outage that slowed them down that was the cause of concern. What worried Patrick was that in the hours when they were not available, no one

---

[3] https://stripe.com/about; accessed on 15 March 2021.
[4] Harry Alford, 'It Never Gets Easier, You Just Go Faster', *Medium*, 28 January 2019. Available at https://medium.com/swlh/it-never-gets-easier-you-just-go-faster-626bafa113e; accessed on 15 March 2021.

had really complained, making them realize that they were not yet important enough. Since then, the brothers have been unstoppable and are trying to fulfil the need that made them create Stripe in the first place. In an interview with Emily Chang of *Bloomberg 1.0* in May 2018, Patrick said that Stripe's goal is 'building a globally unified economic infrastructure that serves companies of every size and makes it possible for way more companies to get started.'[5]

Stripe has seen tremendous growth during the pandemic because the shift to online payments has accelerated. Since March 2020, 200,000 new businesses have signed up with Stripe. Among Stripe's customer base are companies such as Amazon, Slack, Glossier, Shopify, Lyft and Airbnb. Some of Stripe's customers themselves have seen a rapid surge in usage in the past year such as Zoom and Slack. Stripe has also launched several platforms such as Stripe Capital and Stripe Atlas that help other companies borrow money and stay afloat or help new companies register their businesses. By doing this, Stripe has moved from just an online payment portal to finance management. Patrick is also passionate about the cause of climate change. Stripe has launched Stripe Climate, through which online businesses can contribute funds to technologies that remove CO_2 directly from the atmosphere. The Collison brothers have also supported Patrick's alma mater, the University of Limerick, in designing an immersive software engineering programme. In just 10 years, Patrick and John have achieved the seemingly impossible. Patrick feels that there is absolutely no time to waste. He keeps a clock in his office that counts down an estimate of how long he has

---

[5]https://www.bloomberg.com/news/videos/2018-05-31/john-patrick-collison-on-bloomberg-studio-1-0-video; accessed on 15 March 2021.

left to live. It acts as a reminder that old age can come quickly and he needs to make the most of everyday.

Seize the day. Make the most of the time you have.

Most of the principles Stripe is founded on seem to come from Patrick and John's upbringing in rural Ireland. Just like Ireland, which changed from an agrarian economy to a manufacture-based and services economy, Patrick believes that improvement and betterment is possible in every aspect of life. Ireland's joining of the European Union made them more successful in innovation and technology. This taught Patrick the appreciation towards an outward-looking disposition and the realization that it is more productive to be a global organization. Patrick has no delusions of grandeur. In interview after interview, he states that as a company, Stripe is extremely aware of its deficiencies and the areas where they need to improve. This overriding sense of humility seems to define Patrick's character and he is not ashamed to admit that he is terrified of getting too overconfident with Stripe's quick and explosive growth. In 10 years, the company went from 2 to 1,000 employees. The author of the book, *PHP for the World Wide Web*, the book that Patrick had found awesome and that had first inspired Patrick to learn computing, Larry Ullman, is now a Stripe employee too.

A voracious reader, Patrick shares a list of his reading recommendations on his website. The list runs into hundreds of books and is as diverse as his interests. As a child, Patrick's parents took him to the library every day. His parents would often also take the brothers on month-long camping trips, exploring different places in Europe. This opened the Collision brothers up to different kinds of people and different worldviews. Even on the camping trips, the family truck would be loaded with books! Today, Stripe has even started a publishing wing called Stripe Press that publishes books on economic and technological advancement. It is perhaps because of Patrick's interest in varied things that was inculcated in him since childhood that he shares this advice on his website: 'Go deep on things. Become an expert. In particular, try to go deep on multiple things ... One of the main things you should try to achieve by age 20 is some sense for which kinds of things you enjoy doing.'[6]

Read. Explore things in depth.
And try to gain some expertise in it.

What Patrick and John have created with Stripe is not merely a company but a culture. Stripe's office has an open floor plan so people can change desks and get to meet with newer colleagues, gender neutral bathrooms, a transparent email policy and interesting initiatives for any employees who want to become entrepreneurs. Complementing this culture is the humility of the brothers. In fact, in an interview with *BBC*, when asked about experiencing vast wealth at such a young age, John said, 'People now ask this a lot and I feel like they always want some really interesting answer—and I have nothing for them.'[7] Patrick and John shared a modest apartment together in San Francisco for a long time and spent their free time hiking, cycling or studying—John hired a tutor for Law and Patrick for Physics! The brothers also enjoy flying and have been doing so ever since they were teenagers. When Patrick was 19, one summer in Vancouver, he and John spent

---
[6] https://patrickcollison.com/advice; accessed on 15 March 2021.
[7] Will Smale, 'Meet the World's Youngest Self-Made Billionaire', *BBC*, 20 November 2017. Available at https://www.bbc.com/news/business-41859941; accessed on 15 March 2021.

all of the earnings of that summer on learning how to fly. In an interview with *Sunday Times*, Patrick said flying gives a different perspective on the world and appreciation for the world. It is also an interesting form of self-reliance. Extremely self-reliant, Patrick admits, 'I never felt that I was following a track laid down by somebody else.'[8] He surely has charted his own journey, but he makes no fuss about being a pioneer. His opinion is that in life, in the media, and everywhere else, people focus way too much on founders.

Make your own path and set your own trends.

---

[8]https://podcastnotes.org/2018/12/22/collison/; accessed on 15 March 2021.

Chapter 14

BREAKING NEW GROUND

Pierre Omidyar: Founder of eBay

By the time Pierre Omidyar was 29, he was already tired of start-ups. He had been part of quite a few in his 20s and decided it was time to settle down with a regular job. He joined software-maker General Magic, a mobile communication platform company, as a developer relations engineer, while simultaneously making some money on the side freelancing as a web-page designer. Little did he know then that he was to soon launch a company that would change the face of e-commerce.

Interested in technology ever since he was a child, Pierre had initially wanted to study computer engineering. In school, when he first encountered a computer, he learnt how to programme BASIC, often cutting gym class to go and play with a teacher's Radio Shack TRS-80. Rather than punishing him for missing classes, the principal hired him to write his first computer programme for the school library catalogue cards. The programme was used to make a directory of the books and the 14-year-old Pierre earned $6 an hour for it. Self-admittedly not into studies and always way more interested in computers, he once worked on a software programme that would be used to schedule classes and was tempted to put in some code that would ensure he himself didn't have any classes on Friday!

In college, he taught himself to programme the Macintosh with the help of a C programming class called 'Data Structures'. Enrolled into the engineering programme at Tufts University, he found it too rigorous; despite working very hard, he received 25 out of 100 in his chemistry midterm exams. He immediately transferred out of engineering college into liberal arts and enrolled into Computer Science, where he wrote a programme to help Apple Macintosh programmers manage memory, releasing it online as 'Shareware'. Pierre wanted users to pay on the honour system but it did not bring many replies, and the money he expected to get to fund his undergraduate days were spent solely in paying for the post office box.

Later, in 1991, along with three friends, he co-founded a start-up to create pen-computing programmes. Although it failed, the e-commerce site called eShop, which Omidyar introduced on the website, attracted the attention of Microsoft and enticed them to buy the company. Omidyar turned into a millionaire!

No effort and no passion ever goes to waste.

But eShop was not what put Pierre on the map!

Growing up in an atmosphere that encouraged him to try new things, Omidyar had always been curious about the world of online trading and e-commerce. During the Labor Day weekend in 1995, he wrote up a code in Pearl on his home computer that allowed the listing of an item online on sale and then bidding on that item to buy it. The credit for the inspiration behind eBay has also been given to Pamela Wesley, Pierre's then girlfriend, who complained to him about not finding like-minded people on the Internet who would share her passion and interest for collecting pez (an Austrian candy) dispensers. Eager to impress and to help out, Pierre included a small online auction service on his personal webpage to see if online auctions and trading could be arranged from all over the US for collectible items, such as pez dispensers. The very first item sold on the site was a broken laser pointer. Pierre was astonished that anyone would pay for a broken device, but the buyer, Mark Fraser from Canada, was actually interested in it as he enjoyed fixing things. Since then, he has bought over 2,000 items from the site!

Try new things.

By February, the site had become so popular that it outgrew Pierre's personal account. Pierre enlisted his friend, fellow computer programmer Jeff Skoll, to move the site to a new place, and to cover his costs, he charged a few cents to list an item and earned a commission when it was sold. The revenue he earned form the website soon outstripped his salary at General Magic, and Omidyar decided to dedicate his full attention to his new enterprise. Business expanded through word of mouth, and a feedback forum that was added to the site allowed buyers and sellers to rate each other for honesty and reliability.

Pierre tried to register the domain name EchoBay but found that it belonged to a gold-mining company, so he shortened it to eBay, a short form of Electronic Bay Area. By then, of course, the company had already sold one million items. Some of the items listed on the site came as a surprise to Pierre and his colleagues too, like the beanie babies, which brought in $500 million. From collectibles, the site quickly grew, and they started selling a vast range of items, including furniture, electronics, home appliances and vehicles.

The site became so profitable that there was a time when Pierre had to hire part-time help in order to open all the cheques that kept piling up at his door. By the middle of 1997, the website had become one of the most frequented sites on the Internet with more than 150,000 users bidding on nearly 800,000 auctions a day. Pierre said, 'I never had it in mind that I would start a company one day and it would really be successful. I have just been motivated by working on interesting technology.'[1]

> *Work on things that motivate you.*
> *You never know what it could lead to.*

Born in Paris to Iranian parents on 21 June 1967, Pierre and his family moved to the US when he was just a child. Although his parents separated when he was only two, they lived close to each other so that Pierre could build a bond with both. Initially, the family lived in Maryland when his physician father began his residency at Johns Hopkins University Medical Center and his mother taught Persian studies at Georgetown. But Pierre had quite a nomadic childhood, moving every few years, from the Washington area to Hawaii and back again, finally ending up in California where he studied at the University of California, Berkeley, and soon after, joined Claris, a subsidiary of Apple Computer, developing software for Macintosh. As a result of moving frequently while growing up, Pierre was never in one place for long enough to build lasting friendships. So he decided to explore eBay as a tool for community building. In fact, making money was not his primary intent. He really wanted to prove to the world that human beings are inherently trustworthy and nice.

---

[1]https://www.entrepreneur.com/article/197554; accessed on 15 March 2021.

eBay soon became a portal where strangers became friends, shared similar interests, traded with each other, some even finding love and ending up getting married. Like its customers, the company, too, valued human interaction above all else. A case in point is when once, in 1999, the company suffered a service interruption that lasted 22 hours and they took it upon themselves to make 10,000 phone calls to the site's top users to personally apologize and provide them with an assurance for better service in the future.

Personal touch is of the greatest value.

The quick rise of eBay was something the likes of which the world hadn't seen before. Within three years of its establishment, with merely 30 employees, eBay had half-a-million users and was bringing in $47 million as revenue. By the end of the same year, it had reached over a million registered users. On the very first day of trading, the share price nearly tripled, making Pierre an overnight billionaire. By the tenth year of its founding, eBay had acquired giants, such as PayPal and Skype, among many others, and had expanded around the world, employing more than 15,000 people to serve a customer base numbering in the hundreds of millions and operating in 30 countries.

But the accumulation of personal wealth never interested Pierre. In fact, the reticent Pierre even chose to move to Nevada with his wife because they did not want the money-obsessed Silicon Valley to warp their children in any way. Today, the couple live and raise their three children in the Kahala neighbourhood of Honolulu in Hawaii, Pamela's home city. Preferring to stay under the radar and letting his work do all the talking, Pierre admitted in a rare interview with *Honolulu Advertiser* in 2009, 'I do like to fly under the radar. When I walk around town, the only people I want to recognize me and call me by my name are the folks at Starbucks.'[2]

A young Pierre would often accompany his father on his medical rounds on weekends, when they would talk about various subjects. Although he now admits to not finding them all interesting, they did leave a lasting imprint on him and are probably why he finds himself fascinated by a range of things from education, journalism, health, economics, finance, cinema and, of course, what brought him to fame—the Internet. Of his many interests, his primary interest of community building—the main theme behind Pierre's eBay experiment—is also the reason why Pierre and Pamela founded the Omidyar Group in 2004. The Omidyar Group, as its website states, 'is a diverse collection of companies, organizations, and initiatives that strive to catalyze social impact.'[3] The organization, a hybrid structure invested in helping scale innovative organizations to catalyse economic, social and political change, has by now donated over $1.5 billion to non-profit organizations and for-profit companies across multiple investment areas. One of its most noteworthy contributions has been to Pierre's alma mater—Tufts University—in November 2005, a gift of $100 million to endow the Omidyar-Tufts Microfinance Fund. The fund, administered by the Board of Trustees of Tufts University, invests in international microfinance initiatives that are designed to empower people in developing countries to lift themselves out of poverty. Pierre said, 'When you create

---

[2] http://the.honoluluadvertiser.com/article/2009/Mar/22/ln/hawaii903220357.html; accessed on 15 March 2021.
[3] https://www.omidyargroup.com/about/; accessed on 15 March 2021

wealth in a short time, you think about philanthropy as you think about a business.'[4]

Let your work do all the talking.

Always inspired by problems that seem solvable, Pierre decided to give up his executive role in eBay while still in his 30s and focus mainly on his other interests through philanthropic projects. He has put his money where his mouth is and has proved his serious dedication towards philanthropy by signing up for the Giving Pledge along with his wife, resolving to give away 99 per cent of their fortune. His philanthropy is underlined by his entrepreneurial spirit. He admits that the fun thing about being an entrepreneur is to look at the world, see something you don't like and then want to change it.

The Omidyar Group, which aims to bring about social, political and humanitarian change, has a number of organizations and initiatives under its wing, such as the Democracy Fund, Hopelab, Humanity United, Omidyar Network and Ulupono Initiative, and is growing every day. With each initiative, Pierre and his wife have been able to contribute meaningfully to causes that are close to their heart. For instance, some of the main focus areas of the Omidyar Network, which engages in strategic grant-giving alongside impact investing, are to help build courageous leadership and good governance and cultivate informed citizens and thriving communities.

In keeping with his personal goals, Pierre also founded

---

[4] Kate Vinton, 'Billionaire Pierre Omidyar's Foundation Commits $100 Million to Support Investigative Journalism', *Forbes*, 5 April 2017. Available at https://www.forbes.com/sites/katevinton/2017/04/05/billionaire-pierre-omidyars-foundation-commits-100-million-to-support-investigative-journalism/?sh=59a4aeef69f6; accessed on 15 March 2021.

First Look Media and launched the investigative news outfit *The Intercept*, in which journalists including Glenn Greenwald, Laura Poitras and Jeremy Scahill cover national security and surveillance issues brought to light by Edward Snowden. He also produced a film on investigative journalism, *Spotlight*, which won the 2015 Academy Award for best picture for its portrayal of *Boston Globe*'s inquiry into sex abuse by Catholic priests. Since then, he has been a producer of many Hollywood films.

You don't just have to do one thing. Explore all your interests and turn them into opportunities to make a difference.

The reclusive billionaire quietly keeps expanding his evolving portfolio of organizations and programmes, and continues to explore new frontiers for creating positive impact in the world. With every step that he takes, he keeps proving to himself and others that absolutely everything is possible and everything can be done, and that to think of the alternative is dangerous and shows lack of courage. Aptly describing his attitude towards all that he has achieved and keeps accomplishing, Pierre says, 'I was raised with the notion that you can do pretty much anything you want. I always kind of just went ahead and tried things.'[5]

If you try, you can do just about anything.

---

[5] https://www.achievement.org/achiever/pierre-omidyar/#interview; accessed on 15 March 2021.

Chapter 15

CHALLENGING CONVENTIONS

Richard Branson:
Founder of the Virgin Group of Companies

In a letter to his 85-year-old self, about 20 years into the future, Richard Branson wrote: 'Time sure does fly when you're having fun. Keep that blinding sense of optimism that you have had since you were a boy. Remember to always shoot for the moon—even if you miss, you'll land among the stars.'[1]

Ever adventurous, ever ambitious, Richard has always been shooting for the moon and beyond, metaphorically and, in fact, literally. Richard's company Virgin Galactic is the world's first commercial spaceline that is preparing for its first operational flight to space. And Richard intends to be on its maiden voyage. Richard first dreamt of going to space in 1969 when, as a young boy, he watched the moon landing on TV with his family. The possibilities that Neil Armstrong and Buzz Aldrin's adventure opened up to him made him believe that he needed to live life on the edge and live it to the fullest. And that is what he has been doing ever since.

By the time of man's landing on the moon, the then

---

[1] https://www.virgin.com/richard-branson/my-letter-85-year-old-me; accessed on 16 March 2021.

19-year-old Richard had already taken off on his own adventure. Born to Edward James Branson, a barrister, and Eve Branson, a flight attendant, on 18 July 1950 in Surrey, England, Richard Charles Nicholas Branson was the oldest of three siblings. Although quite good at sports, Richard couldn't manage to be good at studies. Born with myopia and dyslexia, he found it extremely hard to cope with the stringent and rigid ways of the educational system in England at the time. He was unable to read, write or spell well and was often beaten for poor behaviour. It was while at Stowe School that Richard and his friend Jonathan Holland-Gems, put off by the strict regulations and rules of the school, started writing to the headmaster with ideas of how things could be improved. The headmaster encouraged them to publish their opinions in the school magazine, but the duo thought their ideas were too revolutionary and hence decided to set up an alternative magazine for it—a space for the youth to express themselves freely. They decided to name it *Student*.

The two ran the magazine from Jonathan's basement and jotted down their business plan—a list of names, potential advertisers and costs—in a school notebook. To print the 50,000 copies of the first edition, they needed a lot of advertising. 'I would clear my throat, lower my voice and try to sound much older and wiser,' Richard says.[2] In the meanwhile, Richard's mother had found a necklace on the road, which she had handed to the police. When no one collected it, the police handed it back to her and she sold it for £100 and gave Richard the money. 'That £100 ended up paving the way for Virgin Galactic, Atlantic and all the other Virgin companies

---

[2] https://www.virgin.com/richard-branson/c-confidence; accessed on 16 March 2021.

around the world today,' says Richard.[3]

In order to keep funding the magazine, Richard thought of starting a mail-order record company with his best friend Nik Powell. While brainstorming names for this new venture, someone suggested 'Slipped Disc'. But the name didn't stick. A friend then suggested 'Virgin', as they were all complete novices at business. This was the beginning of the Virgin brand, which now has more than 40 companies worldwide, employing approximately 60,000 people in 35 countries.

Innovate and be enterprising.

When Virgin Records started doing well, it took over the place of *Student*, which phased out slowly. At the time, post-office workers in England had gone on strike and, unable to get their records delivered to the customers, the duo thought of selling the records from a physical store. They opened one on Oxford Street in London. On Sunday, they handed out leaflets inviting people to buy their cut-price records and on Monday, when the store first opened, there was already a hundred-metre queue outside the shop. Used to moving quickly from one idea to the other, Richard also noticed that there was a need for a residential recording studio. With a large loan from the bank and the help of his family's savings, Richard bought an old manor house some 8 km north of Oxford and turned it into the studio.

One day, a teenage artist called Mike Oldfield played a tape to one of the engineers at the manor, who forwarded it to Richard. Richard was eager to find a record deal for Mike, so moved was he by the beautiful haunting music. After

---

[3]https://www.virgin.com/richard-branson/how-i-started-business-ps500; accessed on 16 March 2021.

approaching six companies and realizing none were willing to sign Mike on, Richard said, 'Screw it, let's start a record company and put it out ourselves.'[4] Mike Oldfield became the first artist for Virgin Records with his album *Tubular Bells*, and Virgin Records became the biggest independent music label in the world, signing artists and bands from Sex Pistols to The Rolling Stones.

Don't depend on others. Do it yourself.

Richard's entrepreneurial journey began as early as when he was 11 years old. With best friend Nik, Richard decided to breed budgerigars to sell them as pets. The venture failed because the birds multiplied faster than they could imagine and, eventually, Richard's mother had to release them. Undeterred, the friends moved on to their next venture. During the Easter holidays, they furrowed the ground and planted 400 seeds that they expected would grow and they could sell around Christmas for £2 each. When they returned home from boarding school, excited about the big fortune they were expecting to make, they realized that rabbits had eaten all the seedlings.

Richard didn't let the early setbacks ruin his enthusiasm for entrepreneurship. He had learnt from his mother, who tried her hand at many projects, from creating wooden tissue boxes to wastepaper bins, that if one idea didn't work, one could always move on to the next. In fact, Richard strongly believes that failure is the most useful lesson of all and is indispensable to the entrepreneurial experience. Later, a number of Virgin enterprises failed as well—from Virgin Cola and Virgin

---

[4]https://www.virgin.com/branson-family/richard-branson-blog/celebrating-45-years-virgin-records; accessed on 16 March 2021.

Cosmetics to Virgin Brides. But all the setbacks in business only made Richard more resilient and more determined. 'If nothing ever fails, then nothing ever improves,' he writes in his blog.[5]

If one idea doesn't work, move on to the next.

For Richard, the greatest business ideas have come from the greatest frustrations. Once, when he and his wife, Joan, were travelling to Puerto Rico, their flight got cancelled. Along with hundreds of other passengers, the Bransons got stranded at a small island airport. Richard quickly tracked down a chartered plane, divided its cost by the number of seats and flew the stranded passengers to Puerto Rico for $39 each. A few months later, a colleague approached him with the idea of starting a transatlantic airline company. Richard, who found other airlines to be lacking in quality, with no entertainment, bad food and unfriendly staff, out of sheer frustration for a quality product decided, 'Let's get a second-hand 747 and give it a go'. And Virgin Atlantic was born.

Branson strongly feels that the only way to enter a market with a product and be successful is if the product is better than its competitors. By 1983, his empire had spread to include over 50 companies and generated combined sales of more than $17 million. With Virgin Atlantic, Branson knew that they were way ahead of their competition, British Airways, because they were able to fill a gap in the market by providing customers with something that would make a real difference to their lives. The birth of Virgin Atlantic in 1984 was followed by the founding of Virgin Australia, Virgin America, Virgin

---

[5]https://www.virgin.com/richard-branson/what-happens-if-we-never-fail; accessed on 16 March 2021.

Holidays, Virgin Limited Edition, Virgin Trains, Virgin Hotels and Virgin Voyages in the travel sector.

> *The greatest ideas can often come
> from the biggest frustrations.*

Delving into multiple areas with equal passion and interest comes from his larger-than-life attitude and his daredevil nature. In a memorable adventurous journey that is his life, two incidents stand out in particular for showcasing Richard's audacity and spirit. The first is in 1987 when he crossed the Atlantic Ocean in a hot-air balloon with Per Lindstrand by his side. The second was a few years later in 1991 when he crossed the Pacific Ocean in a hot-air balloon, breaking the distance and speed records for 10,700 km. He had even attempted to fly around the globe, but after flying over the Himalayas, China and North Korea, Branson and his crew crash-landed in Hawaii on Christmas Day in 1998 and were rescued by US coastguards from shark-infested waters. Turning every experience into a business opportunity, Richard now offers what he calls his 'favourite mode of transport'[6] as an adventure experience to everyone through Virgin Balloon Flights! Every year since 2014, he completes the Virgin Strive Challenge with his family, often hiking, biking, kayaking, climbing some of Europe's biggest mountains and accomplishing extraordinary physical endurance tasks in order to raise funds for Big Change—a non-profit organization set up by his children Holly and Sam to develop innovative education projects that help young people thrive. The 2019 Strive Challenge involved five

---

[6]Richard Branson (@richardbranson), 'Ballooning Is My Favourite Mode of Transport', *Twitter*, 19 September 2019. Available at https://twitter.com/richardbranson/status/1174707218584887297; accessed on 16 March 2021.

days of hiking, swimming, cycling, climbing and paragliding activities in the Alps. Richard endorses the idea that the more we can push ourselves to achieve, the more we will want to achieve.

Every experience can be turned into an opportunity.

In an interview with *CNBC* in July 2019, he said, 'From the very beginning, we set out to create things that we could be proud of and to try to make a difference at Virgin. From founding Student magazine to give [*sic*] young people in the 1960s a voice on issues such as the Vietnam War to creating Virgin Galactic to explore space, we have always tried to do things a little differently and challenge convention.'[7] That he does things differently is an understatement. His daily schedule itself is proof of that. Branson, who lives on his own private island, Necker Island, in the British Virgin Islands, indulges in some form of sport the first thing when he wakes up. Often it is either tennis or his favourite kitesurfing. Incidentally, he holds the record for being the oldest person to kitesurf across the English Channel. His son is the fastest. For six months in a year, he works from his home in Necker, often from his hammock or his sofa or even his bathtub. For the other six, he travels around the world to connect with those who work for the Virgin brand. He doesn't see work and play as two separate things. 'It's all living,' he says.[8] The two things that keep him going and keep him on his feet are lots of tea and his desire

---

[7]Chloe Taylor, 'Richard Branson Says "Stuff" Does Not Bring You Happiness', *CNBC*, 30 July 2019. Available at https://www.cnbc.com/2019/07/30/richard-branson-says-stuff-does-not-bring-you-happiness.html; accessed on 16 March 2021.

[8]https://www.virgin.com/richard-branson/its-all-living; accessed on 16 March 2021.

to live life to the fullest. In his autobiography, cheekily titled *Losing my Virginity*, he wrote about his foray into the airline industry: 'My interest in life comes from setting myself huge, apparently unachievable challenges and trying to rise above them ... from the perspective of wanting to live life to the full, I felt that I had to attempt it.'[9]

> *Work and play are not two separate things.*
> *It's all about living.*

When Richard had told his father that he wanted to drop out of school, he says it required three rounds of walking around the lawn to convince him. Finally, his father, who was ever-loving and supportive, said, 'At least you know what you want to do. Give it a go and if it doesn't work out you can carry on your education.'[10] This motivation stood Richard in good stead for 50 years and he admits that his career has been his education. Not only has he learnt about different industries and how to disrupt them to create change, he has developed interesting new perspectives on many significant issues such as climate change, human rights and drug policy. Not accepting the status quo is his policy in life.

Having started his first charity when he was only 17, Richard now spends most of his time on Virgin Unite, the charitable arm of the Virgin group, through which he has incubated organizations that work towards making people's lives better, whether it be tackling climate change, alleviating global warming, bringing together a group of independent global leaders like Nelson Mandela and Dalai Lama (called

---

[9] Richard Branson, *Losing My Virginity: How I've Survived, Had Fun, and Made a Fortune Doing Business My Way* (1998, Crown Business).
[10] https://www.virgin.com/richard-branson/my-career-was-my-education; accessed on 16 March 2021.

the Elders) who work towards peace and human rights, accelerating the adoption of business solutions to advance the low-carbon economy through the Carbon War Room or creating sustainable economies for the future through the B-Team. It is not a wonder then that he was awarded the title of Knight Bachelor of the Order of the British Empire in the Queen's 2000 New Year Honours list for his services to entrepreneurship.

With most of Richard's businesses being in the sectors that were hit the worst by the pandemic, such as aviation, leisure, hotels and cruises, Richard self-admittedly is facing the most difficult time in his business. Virgin Australia filed for voluntary administration, a form of bankruptcy, and soon after, Virgin Atlantic filed for bankruptcy too. Richard is certain, however, as he admits in a letter to his employees in April 2020, that the Virgin group will come out stronger and kinder after this.[11] Where one area of his business is facing failure, another flies towards success. Virgin Hyperloop, a futuristic, high-speed form of mass transportation, which promises to reduce hours-long trips to minutes, has successfully transported two passengers in a Hyperloop pod. The company hopes to get its safety approval by 2025 and begin commercial operations by 2030. The Virgin brand turned 50 years in 2020 and the fact that it comprises over 40 companies simply goes to show that Richard is not one to call it quits. He says, 'The lesson that I have learned and follow all my life is that we should try and try and try again—but never give up!'[12]

---

[11]https://www.virgin.com/branson-family/richard-branson-blog/an-open-letter-to-virgin-employees; accessed on 16 March 2021.
[12]*Scaling Change*, 'Sir Richard Branson Defines Entrepreneurship', 18 July 2020. Available at https://www.scalingchange.io/post/richard-branson-knight; accessed on 15 March 2021.

Don't stop till you reach your goal.

An avid blogger and storyteller, he writes in one particular blog entry about how, throughout history, dyslexics have imagined and achieved many things that have shaped our world—the most famous being Thomas Edison, Henry Ford and Steve Jobs. Added to the list of those who used their differences to make themselves stand out and create something unique is definitely Richard Branson, known as Doctor Yes, for his ability to take on every challenge with enthusiasm. 'Life is a lot more fun when you say yes! It's amazing how that one little word can lead you on an incredible adventure.'[13] One of Richard's father's most oft-said quotes was, 'Isn't life wonderful?'[14] It indeed is. For Richard and for the lives of all those he has changed through his entrepreneurial adventures, just because he chose to say 'Yes!'

Say yes to opportunities.

---

[13] https://www.virgin.com/richard-branson/y-yes; accessed on 16 March 2021.
[14] https://www.virgin.com/richard-branson/isnt-life-wonderful-lessons-my-dad; accessed on 16 March 2021.

Chapter 16

TREADING NEW GROUND

Sabeer Bhatia: Founder of Hotmail

Sitting in his office at FirePower Systems, in 1994, Sabeer Bhatia and his colleague Jack Smith were trying to email each other about some new technological ideas that they had. But a firewall at the office prevented them from connecting to their personal email on AOL. Not wanting to use the office email for their personal ideas, they had to keep dealing with the frequent hindrance in their communication. Every morning, Sabeer would talk to Jack and tell him yet another story of some guy who'd sold his company for millions. 'Jack! What are we doing here, wasting our lives?'[1] The entrepreneur bug had bit Sabeer and he knew he wanted to do something for which he would be remembered.

One day, when Sabeer was driving home in his red Volkswagen Jetta, Jack called him. He wanted to brainstorm with his friend an idea that he had. Sabeer immediately said, 'Oh my! Hang up that cellular and call me back on a secure line when you get to your house! We don't want anyone to

---

[1] Po Bronson, 'HotMale', *Wired*, 1 December 1998. Available at https://www.wired.com/1998/12/hotmail/; accessed on 16 March 2021.

overhear!'[2] Jack called back after 15 minutes from home and the two discussed in detail an idea about a web-based email that could be accessed from anywhere. Sabeer wrote up a business plan at night and showed it to Jack the next day at office. The night of work left him looking haggard, and when his boss said, 'You've got to cut out the partying, Sabeer,'[3] he simply nodded. Sabeer and Jack did not want to give the game away just yet, realizing that they had possibly struck gold with an idea that could not only solve their own email problems but the problems of many others.

Jack gave up his job to build the idea and Sabeer decided to continue at FirePower and share half of his salary with Jack. As they formalized the product, Sabeer made presentations to possible investors and approached anyone who had money. He pitched to anyone and everyone he could—friends, colleagues, classmates, Texan multimillionaires, oil magnates, real-estate people and even a venture capitalist who funded gas stations. Nineteen venture capitalists turned them down. Instead of looking at the business plan, most only noticed their age— they were only 27!

By then, Sabeer had also begun making a business plan for a web-based personal database called JavaSoft. While working on their email idea, they decided to show JavaSoft as a front to people and kept the actual business plan under wraps for those venture capitalists they trusted and respected. They were wary of someone copying their idea, and to err on the side of caution, even put the JavaSoft name on the front door of their first office in Fremont, California.

---

[2]Po Bronson, 'HotMale', *Wired*, 1 December 1998. Available at https://www.wired.com/1998/12/hotmale/; accessed on 16 March 2021.

[3]Po Bronson, 'HotMale', *Wired*, 1 December 1998. Available at https://www.wired.com/1998/12/hotmale/; accessed on 16 March 2021.

Finally, the venture capitalists Draper Fisher Jurvetson responded to their pitch and asked Sabeer how much money they would need to make their idea happen. Sabeer confidently asked for half-a-million dollars. Draper Fisher Jurvetson settled on $300,000 and Sabeer decided to take it. 'Only in Silicon Valley could two 27-year-old guys get $300,000 from men they had just met. Two 27-year-old guys who had no experience with consumer products, who had never started a company, who had never managed anybody, who had no experience even in software—Jack and I were hardware engineers. All we had was the idea. We didn't have a prototype or even a dummied graphical interface. I just sketched on his whiteboard,' Sabeer said later in an interview with *Wired*.[4]

Have confidence in your ideas.

On 4 July 1996, Jack and Sabeer, along with a team of three full timers and 11 part-timers, finally launched their company HoTMaiL—the uppercase letters spelled out HTML, the language used to write the base of a webpage. They decided to provide their email service for free and obtain revenue through the ads on the website, an idea inspired from Netscape. Within six months—as Sabeer had predicted—HoTMaiL reached one million subscribers.

Born in Punjab, India, on 30 December 1968 to Baldev Bhatia, an officer of the Indian Army, who later joined the Indian Ministry of Defence, and Daman Bhatia, a senior officer at the Central Bank of India, Sabeer had always been a smart kid. With good grades in his schools, The Bishop's School in Pune and St. Joseph's Boys' High School in Bangalore, he

---

[4]Po Bronson, 'HotMale', *Wired*, 1 December 1998. Available at https://www.wired.com/1998/12/hotmale/; accessed on 16 March 2021.

enrolled into an undergraduate degree at the Birla Institute of Technology and Science (BITS) in Pilani. After two years, however, he qualified for a transfer scholarship and moved to California Institute of Technology, being the only applicant in the world in 1988 to get a passing score of 62 to make the transfer possible. He was only 19 and had $250 in his pocket. Having barely used a computer, the young Sabeer landed up at the engineering science department at Caltech, an institute that boasts of 31 Nobel laureates among its alumni and faculty. Sabeer admitted in an interview with *Business Standard*, 'One of the best things I learnt in Caltech was the ability to think on your own.'[5] After Caltech, Sabeer pursued an MS degree in Electrical Engineering from Stanford University. It was also while at Stanford that Sabeer met Steve Jobs, Scott McNealy and other entrepreneurs who hammered in him the confidence: you can do it too.

An angel investor, Farouk Arjani, and also Sabeer's mentor, says about him in *Wired*, 'What set Sabeer apart from the hundreds of entrepreneurs I've met is the gargantuan size of his dream. Even before he had a product, before he had any money behind him, he was completely convinced that he was going to build a major company that would be worth hundreds of millions of dollars. He had an unrelenting conviction that he was not just going to build a run-of-the-mill Silicon Valley company.'[6] Even though Hotmail's user base grew faster than any other company in media history, just within the initial days, they had already run out of their first round of funding.

---

[5]T.E. Narasimhan, 'Life after Hotmail', *Business Standard*, 29 January 2013. Available at https://www.business-standard.com/article/beyond-business/life-after-hotmail-113011900072_1.html; accessed on 16 March 2021.

[6]Po Bronson, 'HotMale', *Wired*, 1 December 1998. Available at https://www.wired.com/1998/12/hotmale/; accessed on 16 March 2021.

Conviction is key.

By the time they hit seven million subscribers, Microsoft took notice. In 1997, Microsoft had six people fly down to Redmond to meet Sabeer. Being an email provider was one area Microsoft had not been able to master and they wanted to acquire Hotmail. To understand what kind of a price they should anticipate, Sabeer took a poll among his investors. Doug Carlisle from Menlo Ventures said $200 million. 'You don't think we can get more than that?' Sabeer asked. 'Sabeer, if you ever reach even my figure, then I'm going to build a life-size bronze sculpture of you and put it in my front lobby,' he said.[7]

Microsoft offered Hotmail $140 million but Sabeer asked for $750 million. Every other week for two months, the team from Microsoft met Sabeer for the negotiations. Often, the negotiators angrily walked out of the meetings. Sabeer's own employees often pressured him to accept the most recent offer and guarantee their security. His venture capitalists, too, urged caution. Sabeer was flown down to Microsoft and shown around its 26 buildings where 25,000 employees worked. In comparison, Hotmail only had 60 employees! Sabeer even met Bill Gates. When Sabeer rejected Microsoft's offer of $350 million, his parents were livid! '$350 million and how much is that in Rupees I can't even put it on my calculator. You accept it right now!' his Dad told him.[8] Colleagues at Hotmail, too, thought Sabeer had lost it. But Sabeer was unwilling to

---

[7] Po Bronson, 'What's the Big Idea?', *STANFORD Magazine*, September/October 1999. Available at https://stanfordmag.org/contents/what-s-the-big-idea; accessed on 16 March 2021.

[8] http://www.meabhi.com/blog/sabeer-bhatia-jaxtrsms-hotmail/; accessed on 16 March 2021.

back down, so sure was he of himself and of his product. He later admitted in jest that he had learnt the art of negotiating from observing the Indian markets, where customers haggled persistently with hawkers while buying vegetables.

Finally, on 30 December 1997, Sabeer's birthday, Microsoft signed the papers and bought Hotmail for $400 million. Doug Carlisle commissioned an artist in Los Angeles to sculpt a bust of Sabeer's as promised.

Know the worth of your idea.

For the first few months after the deal, Sabeer had to pinch himself every day to believe that it was true. His parents, too, didn't believe it and called family friends in the Bay area to confirm the news. Relatives and friends back in India kept calling Sabeer's mother, perplexedly asking what was it that Sabeer sold that earned him a sum of $400 million. Tired of answering, his mother finally replied exasperatedly to one enthusiastic caller, 'Fruit!'[9]

Sabeer's dream, though, didn't end with selling Hotmail to Microsoft. He knew that with Hotmail he had not just built any run-of-the-mill company, but ever optimistic, he was also not happy with building just one product, no matter how huge, and sitting and reaping the benefits that came off it. A technological entrepreneur and a visionary at heart, he kept thinking of new ventures and new ways to solve existing problems. After working for Microsoft for about a year and knowing that he had given to Hotmail everything he could, in April 1999, he left the company to move on to his next project.

---

[9]https://www.youtube.com/watch?v=WOywjAE_gO8; accessed on 16 March 2021.

He forayed into e-commerce with Arzoo. The company failed to succeed initially and suffered like many others with the dot com crash, and Sabeer decided to retire. He spent some time playing golf and travelling all over the world, yet his heart remained in entrepreneurship. So, he relaunched Arzoo again in 2003, this time as a travel portal. In an interview with *The Telegraph*, he said later, 'I thought I had retired. I'll never retire again in my life. It's just the most boring thing on the planet when you have nothing to look forward to, not making your life useful. It seems very nice from the outside, but it's empty.'[10] Arzoo was followed by AMP Technologies, an analytics tool for commercial real estate. Next, Sabeer ventured into the telecom industry, launching a free voice-conferencing product called SabseBolo (translating to 'let's talk to everyone') in 2007. On 14 June 2009, SabseBolo acquired JaxtrSMS, a mobile application that allows users to send free messages. Sabeer hoped that the product that was completely conceived by Indians and developed in India would revolutionize text messaging the same way in which Hotmail revolutionized email. Within less than a month it crossed 700,000 users. Originally operational in four countries—the US, the UK, Canada and Mexico—it soon started providing cheap and efficient service across the globe.

In the same year, Bhatia announced that he was launching a hybrid online–offline Office suite of applications called Live Documents through a company he endorsed called InstaColl. The application competed with well-established cloud offerings such as Google Docs and Microsoft's Office 365. A serial

---

[10]*The Telegraph*, 'I'll Never Retire Again in My Life. It's Just the Most Boring Thing on the Planet', 25 December 2011. Available at https://www.telegraphindia.com/7-days/i-ll-never-retire-again-in-my-life-it-s-just-the-most-boring-thing-on-the-planet/cid/468252; accessed on 16 March 2021.

entrepreneur, even more recently, he was working towards using IoT (Internet of Things) to boost the agricultural sector. As per IBM, IoT has the potential to enable farmers to increase food production by 70 per cent by 2050, and Sabeer believes that this growth will be enabled by the use of technology.

For a while, he was the CEO of a computer software company called Biscuits Lab, and in May of last year, he seems to have founded a stealth start-up that, like its founder, is operating under the radar in stealth mode to avoid public attention. However, knowing Sabeer's creative past and his keenness to keep things under wraps until he is certain his product can create an explosive entry into the market, it can be ascertained that he has something new, interesting and revolutionary up his sleeve.

Sabeer's career is certainly an exemplification of risk-taking and courage. Like all innovators, he has seen highs and lows, with some ideas working and some not. But born with the soul of an innovator and the urge to keep solving problems, he keeps trying. His motto is simple: 'Don't be afraid to tread new ground, but do a sanity test.'[11]

Don't be afraid to explore new territories.

---

[11] https://citatis.com/a23530/121cbd/; accessed on 16 March 2021.

Chapter 17

DARING TO BE DIFFERENT

Sara Blakely: Founder of Spanx

One evening in 1998, Sara Blakely wanted to wear a cream-coloured pair of pants to a party, but she didn't have the right kind of undetectable yet comfortable undergarments to go with it. She decided to cut off the feet of a pair of pantyhose and wear it underneath. It dawned on her that by doing this she had created a new kind of product for women—one for which there was a terrible need in the market. At the time, Sara had a job selling fax machines door to door for an office-supply company called Danka.

On a rather tough day in her life as a saleswoman in Danka, after having been escorted out of buildings several times and having her business card ripped in her face, Sara sat in her car and cried. On returning home that night, she decided to write down her strengths and weaknesses. Under strengths she wrote: sales. Having always wanted to sell something that would help people and change their lives, she wrote down in her journal that she was going to invent a product that she could sell to millions of people and that would make them feel good. Closing her journal, she said out loud, 'Universe give me the idea.'[1] Two years later, she thought of cutting the feet out of her panty hose, which led to a revolutionary idea!

*Have a dream and be determined
about making it come true.*

Sara had never taken a class on business, neither did she have any experience of working in fashion or retail, and so she didn't know where to begin to make her product. Yet she was convinced that it was a good idea and it had to be made! She decided to use the Internet to look up hosiery mills. Most of the hosiery mills, she noticed, were in North Carolina. After trying them on the phone for several months with no luck, she finally decided to take a week off work and drive to North Carolina to find someone she could convince to implement her idea. At each mill, when asked who she worked for, she confidently said 'Sara Blakely' and when asked who was financing her, she said, 'Sara Blakely'. After numerous cold calls with no results, she decided to return to her home in Atlanta. Two weeks after her trip, she got a call from one of the mill owners she had visited. He had decided to make her crazy idea. His daughters had convinced him to have a change of heart because they felt there was a real need for such a product for women.

For a year, Sara worked every night after work and also on weekends on creating a prototype. During that time, she kept her idea under wraps. This gave her the time to actually focus on work rather than wasting it listening to a number of opinions on her future product and wallowing in self-doubt. Only when she was ready to launch did she sit her friends

---

[1] https://www.vanityfair.com/video/watch/how-the-c-e-o-of-spanx-shaped-her-business; accessed on 16 March 2021.

down and explain her product, which she had named Spanx.

Don't indulge anything that can cause self-doubt.

Born to a trial attorney father, John, and an artist mother, Ellen, on 27 February 1971, Sara attended Clearwater High School, where she was also a debater, and graduated from Florida State University, where she was a member of the Delta Delta Delta sorority, with a degree in communication. She wanted to be a lawyer but failed her LSATs twice. Dejected and disappointed, she decided to move to Orlando and try for a job at Disney World. She auditioned for the part of Goofy but being a few inches too short, only got selected to play a chipmunk. Undeterred by failure, Sara then decided to join Danka.

Blakely decided to patent her idea of revolutionary shapewear for women. Wanting a female lawyer who would understand her product, she called the Georgia Chamber of Commerce but was informed that there were no female patent attorneys in Georgia. She went to three different law firms to present her idea and carried her favourite backpack with her for luck. One attorney told her that he had found her idea so implausible that he thought it was a setup by 'Candid Camera'. Those who agreed to help asked for $3,000 to $5,000 to patent her idea. But all she had in savings from her sales job was $5,000. Indomitable, she spent night after night at the Georgia Tech library researching patent law, bought a book called *Patents and Trademarks* from Barnes and Noble and decided to write her own patent.

Don't quit.

She also wanted to package her products well. She wanted it to look different from any of the boring beige she had found in the market, so she made it red and bold. Working with a designer friend, she also put three animated, illustrated girls on the front. But she was clueless about the legal wording on the package, so she bought 10 different kinds of pantyhose from stores, saw what they all had in common on their package, and decided it must be important and, hence, added it to her package too.

Like everything else, Sara orchestrated the advertising and publicity as well. After the prototype was made, she decided to test it on real women. So, she asked her friends and family to try it out. Once the product was launched, she wanted to set things in motion, so she called up all her friends and asked them to buy the products from the stores and even offered to send them a cheque for their efforts.

Fearless and confident, Sara's methods of ensuring her product gets the visibility it deserves is applause worthy. Soon after she had a prototype of her product in hand, she made calls to Neiman Marcus to put it on their shelves. With the prototype in a kitchen Ziploc bag, she flew down to their Dallas office to make a pitch. During the meeting, realizing she was not being able to convince the buyer, she audaciously asked the woman to follow her to the ladies' room where she demonstrated the before and aftereffects of wearing Spanx herself. Within three weeks, Spanx was on their shelves in seven stores. Today, the brand has expanded from women's shapewear to men's shapewear and other clothing items for women too.

Be courageous. Be bold.

Sara's first attempt at business came when she was just out of high school and is a clear indication of the ingenuity that would hold her in good stead later on. She started a babysitting business at an unofficial kids' club at the

Clearwater Beach Hilton, charging $8 a child for a few hours of babysitting while the parents tanned themselves. With no prior experience and no training, she claims to have got away with doing her business for three summers before the hotel closed it down.

A great believer in visualizing her goal, 15 years before Spanx really took off, she had visualized herself on Oprah Winfrey's TV show. When she was dealing with the initial struggles of setting up, she asked the universe for a sign to go ahead. The very same day, Oprah mentioned on her show that she too had been cutting the feet off her pantyhose for years. This was truly the final validation that Sara needed to pursue her idea. In 2000, only two years after starting and before she had even acquired an office space for her company, Oprah Winfrey raved about Spanx on her show. Once the prototype was made, Sara sent Oprah a gift basket with a handwritten note, 'You've been inspiring to me and here, check out my invention.'[2] Andre, who dressed Oprah, put them on her and Oprah loved it so much that she chose it as her favourite product of the year on her show. Soon, Sara got a call from Oprah's show. A crew flew down to Atlanta wanting to film her headquarters, which at the time was just her apartment, since Spanx was yet to acquire an office space. The crew wanted to film her having a staff meeting, so she called the woman who helped mail her products and other friends and asked them to pretend to be the Spanx staff. Oprah endorsed Spanx and the sales took off!

Visualize your success.

---

[2]https://www.inc.com/sara-blakely/how-sara-blakely-got-spanx-on-oprah.html; accessed on 16 March 2021.

By March of 2012, Sara was named the world's youngest, self-made female billionaire by *Forbes* and one of *TIME*'s 100 most influential people. Today, Spanx, with its headquarters in Atlanta, is in more than 50 countries worldwide and Sara herself is currently worth $610 million. Living and leading by example, to budding entrepreneurs, she says, 'Believe in your idea, trust your instincts, and don't be afraid to fail.'[3]

Before seeing actual success, Sara faced innumerable challenges in life. When she was 16, her best friend got run over by a car and was killed in front of her eyes. A few months later, her parents separated. Before her father left, he gifted her a cassette tape series called 'How to Be a No Limit Person' by Wayne Dwyer. Sara believes those tapes changed her life and inspired her to change her mind-set at an early age. It helped her to always listen to her inner voice.

At the Stanford Graduate School of Business where she was invited as a guest, Sarah admitted that many of her ideas come to her because she is hyper-observant and is always asking herself questions. She laughs and admits that she still has 99 pages of ideas that have not been made! It is her perceptive nature and analytical mind that helped her come up with the name Spanx in the first place. For almost a year and a half, she had been thinking of names. During her research she had discovered that products with a strong 'k' sound in their names did really well, as can be seen from Kodak and Coca-Cola, two most recognized products in the market. She had dabbled for a while in stand-up comedy too and a common trade secret was that the 'k' sound was more

---

[3]Kathy Caprino, '10 Lessons I Learned from Sara Blakely that You Won't Hear in Business School', *Forbes*, 23 May 2012. Available at https://www.forbes.com/sites/kathycaprino/2012/05/23/10-lessons-i-learned-from-sara-blakely-that-you-wont-hear-in-business-school/#c2739571438e; accessed on 16 March 2021.

likely to make audiences laugh. One day, while sitting in traffic in Atlanta, the word 'Spanks' just came to her. She had read that made-up words did better as product names and were easier to trademark, so she decided to change the 'ks' to an 'x'. The name still gets her a few laughs, Sara admits.

The Spanx website also carries the fun one liner: 'Don't worry we've got your butt covered.' Even after 18 years of establishing the company, at the Spanx training boot camp, one of the mandatory learning modules for new recruits is comedy. Sara feels that this can help the employees laugh at themselves when they make a mistake and make them unafraid to fail. She herself holds 'Oops Meetings' at the office where she talks about the things she failed at. As a child, Sara's father would often ask her what she failed at that week. He would then go on to congratulate her on her failure. This, Sara claims, redefined failure for her and taught her not to seek validation outside herself.

Don't be afraid of failure.
Failure always leads to better things.

Unafraid and always ready for a challenge, Sara participated in the 2004–5 reality television programme *Rebel Billionaire* hosted by the British entrepreneur and philanthropist Sir Richard Branson. One of the tasks on the show was to climb up the side of a moving hot-air balloon at 10,000 feet to have tea on the top with Branson. Despite her fear of heights, Sara climbed atop the balloon. Although she finished second on the show, Branson was so impressed with her that he gave her $750,000. On the show, Sara had met Nelson Mandela who advised her, 'If you want to change the world, help the women.'[4] So she decided to use the money to establish the Sara Blakely Foundation, a philanthropic organization providing scholarships and grants to aspiring female entrepreneurs. The Foundation, focused mainly on empowering underserved women and girls around the world, has already donated millions. She has donated $1 million to Oprah's Leadership Academy for girls in South Africa and, in 2013, she became the first self-made female billionaire to sign the Melinda and Bill Gates's and Warren Buffett's Giving Pledge, promising to give at least half her wealth to charity. During the pandemic, Sara announced that she would be giving $5 million to support female-run small businesses. The 49-year-old fashion entrepreneur also decided to loan her wedding dress to any brides who had to cancel or postpone their wedding because of the pandemic. Sara feels working for other women is what keeps her going. It is why she started her company in the first place.

On her Instagram page, she defines herself as: 'Mom of 4. Inventor of @SPANX. Love [Popcorn]. Afraid to fly. Refuse to give up my scrunchie. Believe it's my calling to support women.' One post that clearly stands out among all others says, 'No guts, no story'. In another recent post, she mentioned that there is only one thing separating those who dream from those who achieve. 'The difference between people who achieve their dreams, and those who don't is simple. It's about ACTION.'[5] Well, the self-reliant, daring to be different,

---

[4] https://www.youtube.com/watch?v=Nc1p3dOjRPs; accessed on 16 March 2021.
[5] Taylor Locke, 'Spanx CEO Sara Blakely: People Who "Achieve Their Dreams" Have This Trait—"It's Not about Having Brains, Money or Experience"', *CNBC*, 24 November 2020. Available at https://www.cnbc.com/2020/11/24/spanx-sara-blakely-people-who-achieve-their-dreams-have-this-trait.html; accessed on 16 March 2021.

courageous Sara Blakely definitely has the guts and has taken the action that has helped her chart the story of her life and inspire millions.

Dare to be different.

Chapter 18

THE POWER OF PASSION

Steve Ballmer: CEO at Microsoft

Steve Ballmer, a young student at the Stanford Graduate School of Business, living in downtown Palo Alto for a $100 a month, gets a call from a good friend. The friend asks him what he is up to. Steve replies, 'Well, I'm still in school.' The friend says, 'Oh, too bad, too bad you don't have a twin brother ... we could really use you,' and then he hangs up.[1] The friend was Bill Gates and this was the first time he had expressed interest in having Steve Ballmer join him in his new start-up, Microsoft.

Steve and Bill had first met at Harvard University through common friends. They lived down the hall from each other. Realizing that that they had both ended up skipping a course, they bonded over the fact that they were in a lot of trouble for it. Bill said in an interview that cramming together for an advanced Economics exam was a determining event in their friendship. The young college students who could relate to each other and discuss typical college angst ended up becoming very good friends. Diametrically opposite personality types, they found comfort around each other as one complemented

---

[1] *Wall Street Journal*, 'Scenes From a Marriage', 9 June 2008. Available at https://www.wsj.com/articles/SB121261284347446273; accessed on 16 March 2021.

the other, and relied on each other for emotional support. Playing poker and watching movies like *Singin' in the Rain* and *A Clockwork Orange* were only some of their other special shared memories.

When Bill dropped out of Harvard to start Microsoft, Steve was headed towards a more academic path. He graduated magna cum laude in Math and Economics and took up a job at Proctor and Gamble as an assistant product manager, where he was in-charge of the Duncan-Hines's Moist & Easy cake mixes. Though their paths had diverged, the friends stayed in touch. One summer, Steve even visited Bill in Albuquerque. After two years at Proctor and Gamble, Steve enrolled at the Stanford Business School. His goal was simple: to get a job in a big company. That's when the call came from Bill. Steve, who discovered he had an interest in business as a sophomore, understood Bill's cryptic message and called him back the very next day. 'I don't have a twin brother, but how about me?' he asked.[2] On 11 June 1980, five years after Microsoft had been founded, Steve dropped out of business school and joined Microsoft as employee no. 24.

Embrace every opportunity that comes your way.

Born to Beatrice Dworkin and Frederic Henry Ballmer on 24 March 1956, Steve and his sister Shelly grew up in the US, in the suburbs of Detroit in Farmington Hills. Steve's father had been an interpreter for the war crime trials in Nuremberg and immigrated to the US through his language skills. In the US, he worked as a hotel lobby receptionist, a payroll clerk and an assembly line worker until finally he became a mid-level

---

[2] *Wall Street Journal*, 'Scenes From a Marriage', 9 June 2008. Available at https://www.wsj.com/articles/SB121261284347446273; accessed on 16 March 2021.

manager at Ford Motor Company. Steve had always been a bright student. He attended the Detroit Country Day School on a scholarship and scored a 4.0 grade point average. He was also on the football and track teams, managed the basketball team and participated in various school clubs. He graduated with a perfect score of 800 on the Math section of the SATs. That he would go to Harvard was not a surprise to his parents. In fact, ever since he was eight, Steve's father knew that his son would one day go to Harvard. At Harvard, too, Steve was passionately involved in a number of things. Not only was he an exemplary student, he also worked on the *Harvard Crimson* newspaper and the university literary magazine and managed the football team. Of their time working together, Bill said that Steve would participate in everything on campus and keep himself really busy.

But Steve had not always been enthusiastic and hyperactive. As a child, he struggled with shyness and would often hyperventilate before attending Hebrew School. His mother, to calm him down, would make him take short breaths. Today, one look into Microsoft's history can tell us about how Steve's energetic nature and electric personality, his passion and enthusiasm, drove the organization towards unprecedented success. Steve is known especially for his raw displays of emotion and his legendary motivational, emotional and over-the-top speeches at Microsoft where he high-fives people, cheers the crowd and often even jumps around the stage. In one famous and oft-cited example, Steve is seen animatedly chanting 'Developers! Developers! Developers!' at a presentation on Microsoft's twenty-fifth anniversary. Not afraid to be himself, in 1991 at a meeting in Japan, he even ended up damaging his vocal cords by excitedly screaming 'Windows!'[3]

When Steve told his parents he wanted to drop out of Stanford to join Microsoft, they did not seem to take it too well. He recalled in an interview that his father asked, 'What the heck is software?', while his mother was concerned, 'Why would a person ever need a computer?'[4] Steve had promised them that if his stint at Microsoft did not work out, he would go right back to business school and follow the more conventional path of becoming an academic. He never did have to go back.

At Microsoft, Steve started out by being an assistant to Bill but became the first business manager that Microsoft had. He joked in an interview with *CNBC*, 'I was Bill's assistant basically: chief cook and bottle washer.'[5] Microsoft needed someone who would be able to deal with the challenges of running a growing business and who knew about hiring, finances and people management. Steve, probably the only non-engineer in the company at the time, fit the role perfectly. Steve had made himself indispensable to the company and to Bill. He had the ability to identify potential talent, which helped Microsoft grow. Bill later admitted in an interview that Steve taught him 'how to hire lots of people—really good people—and create organizations

---

[3]https://www.youtube.com/watch?v=Vhh_GeBPOhs; accessed on 16 March 2021.
[4]Zameena Mejia, 'How Steve Ballmer Went from Making $50,000 a Year as an Assistant at Microsoft to Becoming a Billionaire', *CNBC*, 27 July 2018. Available at https://www.cnbc.com/2018/07/27/billionaire-steve-ballmer-started-out-making-only-50000-at-microsoft.html; accessed on 16 March 2021.
[5]Zameena Mejia, 'How Steve Ballmer Went from Making $50,000 a Year as an Assistant at Microsoft to Becoming a Billionaire', *CNBC*, 27 July 2018. Available at https://www.cnbc.com/2018/07/27/billionaire-steve-ballmer-started-out-making-only-50000-at-microsoft.html; accessed on 16 March 2021.

and teams.[6] Bill offered him a salary of $50,000 and an equity stake of 5 to 10 per cent in the company and 10 per cent of the profit growth he generated.

Don't be afraid to start out small.

In 1980, soon after joining the team, Steve helped purchase the Disk Operating System (DOS) from a small organization in Seattle. This became the foundation for Microsoft's star product—MS-DOS. His next big venture was helping negotiate and land a landmark deal with IBM to get them to run MS-DOS on their machines. IBM's goal was to make computers available to everyday people, and with Microsoft's MS-DOS, this became a reality.

During his tenure, he also oversaw the team that produced the Windows operating system. Under his leadership, Microsoft launched the Xbox and entered the search engine market with Bing. In 2011, Steve helped Microsoft make their largest acquisition in history—an $8.5 billion acquisition of the Internet communication company Skype. Like Bill, Steve was motivated by one dream: to make Microsoft grow and control every aspect of the software industry.

By 1986, when Microsoft became a publicly held company, the not-yet-30 Steve became a multimillionaire. From 1980 to 1998, he headed several divisions and held different executive titles at the company. An outgoing leader known for his passionate and high-energy behaviour, Steve led the business side of the organization, which grew by leaps and bounds. In July 1998, Bill asked him to become the president,

---

[6]Zameena Mejia, 'Bill Gates Tells Harvard Students He Struggled to Quit This Bad Habit to Make Sure Microsoft Was a Success', *CNBC*, 10 May 2018. Available at https://www.cnbc.com/2018/05/10/bill-gates-quit-this-bad-habit-to-get-microsoft-off-the-ground.html; accessed on 16 March 2021.

and in January 2000, he was named CEO, a position Bill had held since the inception of the company. Bill trusted Steve completely and Steve was extremely loyal to Bill. As Microsoft grew, their friendship became stronger. Under Steve's leadership, Microsoft saw and overcame multiple challenges but also recorded a phenomenal increase in profits with the annual revenue surging from a $25 billion to $70 billion.

Nurture friendships and be loyal.

Microsoft became Steve's life. It was like a fourth child, he would admit jokingly. Steve and his wife Connie Snyder have three sons. They had first met and fallen in love at Microsoft and married in 1990. After 15 years of being the CEO, Steve was visibly emotional when he gave his last speech at his retirement. With tears streaming down his face, he said, 'You work for the greatest company in the world, soak it in.' His message was clear in the song he picked out to end his speech: 'I've Had the Time of My Life'.[7]

The mathematically gifted Steve always thought of sports as a medium of communication. A lineman in his days at the Detroit Day School, Steve still gets excited at the memory of wearing jersey no. 71—the same number as his hero, Detroit Lions defensive tackle Alex Karras. The year he retired, he acquired the NBA's Los Angeles Clippers for $2 billion. At the Milken Global Conference in Beverly Hills, Steve said, 'I loved running Microsoft, but basketball is a whole different notion. The burst of adrenaline you get is really different. Boom. Every 24 seconds. Did we score? Boom. Did we win? Sports has a high accountability culture. In software, you

---

[7]https://www.theverge.com/2013/9/27/4779036/exclusive-video-steve-ballmers-intense-tearful-goodbye-to-microsoft; accessed on 16 March 2021.

assign someone to fix a problem. In business, we say we'll get to it tomorrow. In sports, it's just over.[8] Incidentally, it was Paul Allen, Microsoft's other co-founder, who convinced Steve to invest in a basketball team. Allen had rightly predicted that Steve would love it.

To attend games, he commutes from his home in Seattle by private jet, explaining, 'Time is our most precious commodity, and there are conveniences that wealth brings to essentially get you more time.'[9] But, Steve refrains from outward shows of wealth. He still remains the passionate, enthusiastic Midwestern who attends the practice sessions and retrieves basketballs for the players during drills. Doc Rivers, the Clippers' coach, said in an interview, 'He's the most normal $24 billion guy I know.'[10]

Steve is no typical billionaire. Hardworking and dependable, his primary thought after retirement is what to do with all of the wealth. Once, when asked what being rich feels like by MBA students at USC, Steve replied, 'It's sort of a privilege, sort of a duty, sort of a burden. How do I make a difference?'[11]

---

[8]Dean Takahashi, 'Steve Ballmer on Life after Microsoft', *VentureBeat*, 1 May 2018. Available at https://venturebeat.com/2018/05/01/steve-ballmer-on-life-after-microsoft/; accessed on 16 March 2021.

[9]Karen Crouse, 'Steven A. Ballmer Speaks Loudly and Carries a Big Wallet', *The New York Times*, 21 April 2015. Available at https://www.nytimes.com/2015/04/22/sports/basketball/steven-a-ballmers-inner-fan-finds-its-voice-in-a-corner-of-the-nba.html; accessed on.

[10]Karen Crouse, 'Steven A. Ballmer Speaks Loudly and Carries a Big Wallet', *The New York Times*, 21 April 2015. Available at https://www.nytimes.com/2015/04/22/sports/basketball/steven-a-ballmers-inner-fan-finds-its-voice-in-a-corner-of-the-nba.html; accessed on 16 March 2021.

[11]Karen Crouse, 'Steven A. Ballmer Speaks Loudly and Carries a Big Wallet', *The New York Times*, 21 April 2015. Available at https://www.nytimes.com/2015/04/22/sports/basketball/steven-a-ballmers-inner-fan-finds-its-voice-in-a-corner-of-the-nba.html; accessed on 16 March 2021.

Don't be carried away by wealth. Try to make a difference.

To make a difference and leave a personal legacy through philanthropy, Steve and Connie formed the Ballmer Group, an organization that focuses on fighting racial and economic inequality and helping children and families escape the cycle of poverty. The group has launched economic mobility and anti-poverty programmes across the US with a $60 million setup. The Ballmer Group has donated more than $300 million in the last three years to fund the work of more than 70 non-profits working in communities of colour in Detroit, Seattle and Los Angeles. One of their most significant political contributions has been giving $7 million to a political action committee connected to a national gun control group co-founded by former New York City mayor Michael Bloomberg. Steve also founded the non-profit, non-partisan website *USAFacts* in 2019 as a free public service to help make government data more accessible. This became especially helpful during the pandemic when the organization launched the 'Coronavirus Impact and Recovery Hub' to track the government's data, especially on specific issues such as how employment statistics compared to health statistics in communities across the country.

Like at his NBA games, Steve has also been a great, and probably the greatest, cheerleader for Microsoft. One needs to be the first and most critical user of one's own products, even before customers are subjected to them, he feels. Loyal and devoted, he still owns Microsoft stocks and drives a Ford car. In an interview with *Business Insider*, Steve had once said that the best advice he has ever got is from his father who told him, 'If you're going do a job, do a job. And if you're not going to do a job, don't do a job. And that is the key of everything.'[12] Steve lived by this advice all his life and put his heart, soul and mind into his work for Microsoft. It's no wonder then that he was the first person Bill Gates trusted to take care of his brainchild Microsoft after he stepped down.

Put your heart, soul and mind into your work.

---

[12]Julie Bort, 'This Was the Best Advice Steve Ballmer Ever Got', *Business Insider*, 8 March 2014. Available at https://www.businessinsider.com/the-best-advice-steve-ballmer-ever-got-2014-3/commerce-on-business-insider; accessed on 16 March 2021.

Chapter 19

TURNING OPPOSITION INTO OPPORTUNITY

Varun Agarwal: Author; Filmmaker; Founder of Last Minute Films, Alma Mater, Grades Don't Matter

Varun Agarwal once wrote a post on his Facebook page:

Myth: If it's meant to be, it will happen.
Reality: If it's meant to be, *you* have to make it happen.[1]

And he did make it happen! He started three companies, became a published author, a filmmaker and motivational speaker all before he turned thirty.

Brought up in a typical middle-class Indian society where emphasis is always on education and job security, where risk-taking is usually discouraged and where success is measured by ticking off check boxes of job, marriage and children by the age of 30, Varun always thought a little differently. His parents, like most Indian parents, wanted their son to become an engineer. Although his heart was not in it, he decided to give it a shot and pursued an engineering degree in Telecommunications from CMR Institute of Technology. Despite being an above-average student, he failed for the first time at engineering.

---
[1] https://www.facebook.com/varun760/; accessed on 16 March 2021.

The failure gave him a sense of freedom. Ignoring the noise of what society said around him, he decided to pursue what he had always wanted to do—filmmaking. So he picked up his handycam and started shooting. Varun had first discovered his passion for filmmaking when he was in the eleventh grade. His first video was one of a school road trip. This time around, he decided to put his videos up on the newly launched content-sharing platform, YouTube. In 2005, while still in engineering college, he started his first company, Last Minute Films, an indie film production company focused on producing music videos, corporate films and ad films. The inspiration behind the name came from his observation of how everything and anything remarkable always happened at the last minute. Later, he realized the same holds true for life as well seeing as life doesn't always give us time to prepare for everything.

Varun's videos became very popular, and soon, he became one of the finalists for a video contest announced by VH1 for Pentagram, one of India's first indie bands. Although his video didn't win, Pentagram liked it. And with their blessing, Varun uploaded it on YouTube. The video ended up getting 100,000 views and was played on VH1 51 times a day. A production company in Mumbai took notice of the video and flew Varun down to offer him a full-time job to direct. Varun was only 20 and still enrolled as an engineering student.

Make it happen.

Surer than ever of not wanting to pursue engineering, and instead wanting to become a filmmaker, Varun braved telling his parents about his decision. His parents were not convinced and he was asked to return to Bengaluru and get his engineering degree. Fighting through one more year of college, Varun finally got his degree.

All his life, ever since he was a kid, Varun had been used to thinking a lot before making any decisions, before taking any steps. By the time he got out of college, he decided that thinking, and especially overthinking, hadn't taken him anywhere. He decided to not think and just do what his heart told him to. To the chagrin of his parents, neighbours and relatives, Varun bought a one-way bus ticket to Mumbai to become a director. Soon after, he was directing videos for Phat Phish Productions in Mumbai. Within a few days of joining, he found himself in Chennai directing the Oscar-winning music director A.R. Rahman in a video. A few weeks later, he was directing the famous Indian actress Preity Zinta in a music video for a song by Shankar–Ehsaan–Loy.

Only 20, and self-admittedly looking like 14, Varun was often not taken seriously as a director as people refused to believe that this young boy was actually the one calling the shots. Varun recalls how, during one shoot, just to motivate himself, he had to lock himself in the men's room and give himself a 20-second pep talk, a technique that he had picked up from a book that mentioned that if you are brave enough to follow through a commitment in the first 20 seconds, you can stick to it for a lifetime.

Later, pep talks kind of became Varun's thing. And now, he is a motivational speaker, having given talks all over the world. His talks and videos have been seen by over 10 million people globally and he has a following of over half-a-million people. Some of his most notable talks in India have been at the headquarters of Google India, Cisco India, Yahoo India and HP India, besides many IITs, IIMs and over 100 colleges across India. During his talk at IIT Bombay, Varun realized that even in a premier institution where one would assume the students are clear about their future path, they are really still seeking answers. His story of struggle resonated with young millennials throughout the country. At the Ink Conference in 2013, where Varun's speech ended up getting over 500,000 views in just four days, he ended with the message of how we should always live a life that we want to live and not one which someone else wants us to live. His mantra remains the same: 'Don't overthink and follow your dreams.'[2]

Follow your instinct and don't overthink.

One day in 2009, back from his directorial stint on Mumbai, Varun met up with an old friend Rohn Malhotra from his school, Bishop Cotton, at Bengaluru's oldest pubs, Noon Wines. The friends reminisced about old days and spoke of school and 'adulting' and complained about the drudgery of nine-to-five jobs that they felt society would inevitably expect them to be a part of. Fuelled by pitchers of draught beer and bound by nostalgia for their school, the 20-somethings suddenly had an idea. How would it be if they had hoodies with the word 'Cottonian' on it? The duo jotted their idea down on a napkin and, inhibition-free and willing to take risks, decided to turn it into a business idea.

The entrepreneur in Varun had been waiting to rear its head for a very long time. He first experienced entrepreneurship when he was only in fourth grade at Bishop Cotton School. His mother, Purnima, had baked him some brownies for school. Realizing that many of the boys at school liked it, he decided to make a business of it and, with the money, he wanted to

---

[2]Nikita Puri, 'Varun Agarwal, from Hoodies to Bollywood', *Business Standard*, 15 December 2017. Available at https://www.business-standard.com/article/beyond-business/varun-agarwal-from-hoodies-to-bollywood-117121501531_1.html; accessed on 16 March 2021.

buy his mother a present. He was becoming quite successful until the teacher found out and shut it down.

This time round, he was determined to make his business work. After designing the logo, Varun and Rohn found a friend who offered to make them some samples. They then went to the Old Boys' Day event at Bishop Cotton and put up a stall, hoping that people would be interested. Within the very first day, they sold 2,500 hoodies. Students spread the word and soon other schools and colleges wanted similar merchandise too! Operating from a garage, the duo launched their company, Alma Mater, online, with seed capital of only ₹1 lakh, and started to cater to schools and colleges across India.

Start somewhere. Anywhere.

Like most start-ups, the initial days for Alma Mater were not full of glamour and glory. Most concerned about his venture were Varun's mother and the 'well-wishers' who were always poking their noses in Varun's life, repeatedly belittling him and mocking him for his lack of ambition and for not becoming an engineer of worth. Varun, in jest, and perhaps, even in seriousness, refers to this symbolic epitome of well-wishers as 'Anu Aunty'. Like him, he knows all youngsters in India have an Anu Aunty, who seem too concerned about their future but really are negative powers that prevent them for doing what they want in life. Anu Aunty even went as far as to call Varun just a T-shirt salesman!

By now, used to the idea of failing and knowing that it wasn't really the worst that could happen, Varun took to Facebook and social media to publicly encourage himself and others like him and to face the proverbial 'Anu Aunties' in society. Such was the success of his pep talks and pep posts that it encouraged a huge number of his followers, most of whom were young people in new India who often felt forced to take up career paths just because of societal and parental pressures and were unable to follow their own dreams through. Encouraged to write a book about it but not knowing whether he had it in him, Varun thought of testing the merit of his writing by sending a few of his blogs to a publishing house, Rupa Publications. The publisher liked it, and soon, Varun had a book deal in his hands. He wrote the book, *How I Braved Anu Aunty and Co-Founded a Million Dollar Company* in eight days, while under house arrest as a result of being ill.[3] Within a month of its release in 2012, it became a national bestseller and, today, has sold over half-a-million copies.

With the book, Varun had managed to turn his greatest adversary—Anu Aunty—into his brand ambassador. He also proved that the theories he had been made to believe all his life—'think before you do anything' and 'look before you leap'—didn't really work, and sometimes, it was best to not think and just take the leap.

Turn every opposition into an opportunity.

By then, Varun had already co-founded another company— Reticular, a social media marketing organization—and Alma Mater was also thriving, having become India's largest customized merchandise company for schools, colleges and corporates, growing to a million dollars in revenue, being funded twice by the Indian Angel Network. Varun and Rohn found themselves on the covers of the biggest magazines and in over 50 newspaper articles. A year after starting

---

[3]https://www.rediff.com/getahead/report/slide-show-1-career-most-indian-pulp-fiction-authors-write-terrible-english/20120816.htm; accessed on 16 March 2021.

the company, Varun and Rohn were back in the same pub, chatting away as usual when they saw a young boy walk past them wearing an Alma Mater hoodie with 'Cottonian' written on it. Life seemed to come full circle! This, Varun admits, is easily one of the best moments of his life.

Varun's semi-autobiographical novel soon became an inspiration for youngsters, many of whom started their own company after reading it. He once also had a woman call him crying as her son wanted to commit suicide because he felt she didn't understand him. Reading Varun's book, the mother said, helped her reconnect with her son and understand his struggles. Today, Varun feels that we need to encounter more Anu Aunties in society because they represent the challenge that one must face and overcome in order to find their dreams and become successful.

In 2018, with six others, he started his fourth company, Grades Don't Matter, which encourages young people to be creative and innovative by disrupting education. The company, which didn't succeed the first time around and was relaunched, conducts courses on a range of subjects from public speaking to beatboxing. To teach these courses, Varun has brought on board the best in the business; from director Nitesh Tiwari to author Amish Tripathi, from producer Siddharth Roy Kapur to entrepreneur and founder of Oyo, Ritesh Agarwal. The company vows to bridge the gap between degree and skills. Inspired from Varun's life, where his engineering degree did not help him find his career path, Grades Don't Matter aims to aid people with the right skills that are not taught in conventional schools and colleges, so that they can follow their dreams.

Through his speeches, his many companies, and his social media pages, Varun keeps motivating and inspiring young people to follow their dreams and make a difference. After all, as Varun says in his book, quoting his mentor Steve Jobs, 'We're here to put a dent in the universe. Otherwise why else even be here?'[4]

Make your mark. Put a dent in the universe.

---

[4]Varun Agarwal, *How I Braved Anu Aunty and Co-founded a Million Dollar Company* (2012, Rupa).

Chapter 20

KEEPING IT SIMPLE

Warren Buffett: Founder of Berkshire Hathaway

Warren Buffett once said, 'I always knew I was going to be rich. I don't think I ever doubted it for a minute.'[1] When Buffett was young, he had apparently said that he would be a millionaire by age 30 or jump off the tallest building in Omaha. As of 2020, his estimated net worth is $85.6 billion. Today he is known as the Oracle of Omaha because he still continues to live in Omaha where he grew up and because his investment prowess is so well known that everyone follows his investment choices very closely. In fact, the reputation of the head of Berkshire Hathaway, the multinational conglomerate holding company, as a businessman is so good that if it is known that he was to buy a stock of a certain company, its price would shoot up by 10 per cent. In 1962, when Buffett first started buying shares of Berkshire Hathaway, it was only a textile company. Under him, it has diversified into a range of industries. Today, it has substantial minority stock holdings in some of the biggest and

---

[1] Ethel Jiang, 'Here Are the 21 Most Brilliant Quotes from Warren Buffett, the World's Most Famous and Successful Investor', *Markets Insider*, 12 February 2020. Available at https://markets.businessinsider.com/news/stocks/warren-buffett-21-best-quotes-2019-2-1027944381#-i-always-knew-i-was-going-to-be-rich-3; accessed on 17 March 2021.

best-known publicly traded companies in the US, including Coca-Cola, Kraft Heinz, IBM, American Express and Wells Fargo. It also owns numerous private companies such as Geico, McLane Company and Burlington Northern Santa Fe, among others. And it is the world's largest financial company by revenue.

Buffett bought his first stock when he was just 11 with $114.75 that he had saved since the first grade. He bought three shares of Cities Services Preferred at $38 per share. The price of the shares dropped to $27 and then rose up again to $40. That's when Buffett sold the shares to make a marginal profit. Ultimately, though, the stocks soared to nearly $200 per share. This experience taught him a lesson for life: Patience.

If you aspire for greatness, learn to be patient first.

Born to Howard Buffett and Leila Stahl Buffett on 30 August 1930, in Omaha, Nebraska, love of stocks was in Warren's DNA. Howard initially worked as a stockbroker and Warren would often visit the stockbrokerage shop as a child and chalk in the stock prices on the blackboard in the office. Often referred to as mathematical prodigy for his ability to add large columns of numbers in his head, Warren was so interested in Math that he asked his father to take him to the New York Stock Exchange on his first visit to New York when he was only 10 years old. The only other two things that he wanted to see in New York were the Scott Stamp and Coin Company and the Lionel Train Company. The visit to the New York Stock Exchange turned out to be his 'aha' moment and that's when he decided, as early as at the age of 10, that he wanted to dedicate his life to making money.

Buffett's entrepreneurial interests kicked in very early. At the age of five, he was selling Chiclet gum outside his house on the sidewalk. He also sold lemonade but outside his friend's house because there was more traffic there. At six, he bought six packs of Coca-Cola from his grandfather's grocery shop for $0.25 and sold each bottle for a nickel, making a five-cent profit. Some of his other entrepreneurial ventures were buying used golf balls for $3.50 and selling them for $6, selling collectible stamps and even rummaging through discarded horserace betting tickets in search for winners and turning them in for the pay-out. By the time he was 13 and already sure about his dreams of making money, he took a job delivering copies of the *Washington Post*. On his routes, he tracked which homes had expiring magazine subscriptions and sold them new subscriptions. This media distribution business turned out to be so successful that by 15, he had made $2,000 and decided to invest $1,200 in a 40-acre farm, where he had a profit-sharing agreement with a Nebraskan farmer. He also filed tax returns for the first time that year, claiming his bike as a $35 tax deduction.

Set a goal to make money.

In 1942, Howard Buffett was elected to the US House of Representatives. The Buffett family moved to the D.C. area where Warren first attended the Alice Deal Junior High School and then moved to the Woodrow Wilson High School. In high school, his entrepreneurial activities continued. In 1945, in his sophomore year, along with his friend Don Danley, Warren started a lucrative pinball business. The duo purchased a used pinball machine for $25. They installed it in a barbershop, and within a few months, with the profits, they bought and installed pinball machines in three other locations. A year later, he sold the business for $1,200. His friends and peers recognized his talent and his high school yearbook photo caption rightly said: 'Likes math; a future stockbroker.'[2]

Buffett's upbringing had instilled in him a great sense of ambition and creativity, and by the age of 16, he had amassed a fairly large fortune. As a result of this, and probably knowing fairly well that he would continue with yet more business ventures, he didn't see the point of going to college. But when his father, whom Warren revered, insisted, he enrolled at the University of Pennsylvania to study business. After two years, he moved to the University of Nebraska. Although not too keen on college initially, Buffett had his heart set on one college in particular: Harvard Business School. But he faced his first major setback when he was rejected just 10 minutes after the interview. He was told, 'Forget it. You're not going to Harvard.'[3] He didn't let this first setback or even later ones in his career, especially those resulting from the recent pandemic, bring him down. He aptly stated in *Financial Times* once: 'If you played golf and you hit a hole in one on every hole, nobody would play golf, it's no fun. You've got to hit a few in the rough and then get out of the rough ... That makes it interesting.'[4] In retrospect, the rejection from Harvard turned out to be the best thing that happened to him.

Rejection is often the best thing that can happen to you.

---

[2] J.K. Lasser, *Pick Stocks like Wareen Buffet*: What You Can Learn from the Best Investor of Our Time (2001, Sage), p.19.

[3] Kathleen Elkins, 'Warren Buffett: Getting Rejected by Harvard Was the 'Best Thing that Ever Happened to Me', *CNBC*, 31 January 2017. Available at https://www.cnbc.com/2017/01/31/hbs-rejection-was-the-best-thing-that-ever-happened-to-warren-buffett.html; accessed on 17 March 2021.

[4] Robert Armstrong, Eric Platt and Oliver Ralph, 'Warren Buffett: 'I'm Having More Fun than Any 88-Year-Old in the World', *Financial Times*, 25 April 2019. Available at https://www.ft.com/content/40b9b356-661e-11e9-a79d-04f350474d62; accessed on 17 March 2021.

Once, when asked about the key to his success, Buffett pointed to a huge stack of books and said, 'Read 500 pages like this every day. That's how knowledge works. It builds up, like compound interest.'[5] He spends about 80 per cent of his day reading. In an interview with *TIME*, he discussed the way he spends his day: 'I read and think ... I do more reading and thinking and make less impulse decisions than most people in business. I do it because I like this kind of life.'[6] The book that changed the course of his life and taught him about intellectual framework for investing he picked up when he was 19. It was a well-known book in the Wall Street world called *The Intelligent Investor* written by Ben Graham. On hearing that Graham, whom Buffett considers the second biggest influence on his life after his father, and David Dodd, another of his idols, were both professors at Columbia Business School, Buffett sent out a letter in mid-August. 'I said, "Dear Professor Dodd. I thought you guys were dead, but now that I found out that you're alive and teaching at Columbia, I would really like to come." And he admitted me.'[7]

Read, read and read.

Buffett's second biggest rejection came when, after graduating from Columbia in 1951, he asked Ben Graham if he could

---

[5]Kathleen Elkins, 'Berkshire Hathaway Star Followed Warren Buffett's Advice: Read 500 Pages a Day', *CNBC*, 27 March 2018. Available at https://www.cnbc.com/2018/03/27/warren-buffetts-key-tip-for-success-read-500-pages-a-day.html; accessed on 17 March 2021.

[6]Chris Winfield, 'This Is Warren Buffett's Best Investment Advice', *TIME*, 23 July 2015. Available at https://time.com/3968806/warren-buffett-investment-advice/; accessed on 17 March 2021.

[7]Kathleen Elkins, 'Warren Buffett: Getting Rejected by Harvard Was the 'Best Thing that Ever Happened to Me', *CNBC*, 31 January 2017. Available at https://www.cnbc.com/2017/01/31/hbs-rejection-was-the-best-thing-that-ever-happened-to-warren-buffett.html; accessed on 17 March 2021.

work for his company and was turned down. Buffett moved back to Omaha and sold securities for his father's brokerage firm Buffett-Falk & Co. till Graham had a change of heart and called him back to New York. When Graham closed his partnership in 1956, Buffett moved back to Omaha and with all the knowledge he had gathered, started his own company Buffett Partnership Ltd. By the end of the '50s, Buffett had opened seven partnerships.

In a speech many years later at Columbia, Buffett advised, 'You will move in the direction of the people that you associate with.'[8] Sharing the stage with him at the time was one of his closest friends, whom Buffett claims he has learnt a lot from—Bill Gates. The two, who spend a lot of time together talking, eating out, and playing Bridge, also have one more thing in common: they both believe in using their fortunes to help the world. In 2010, their started the Giving Pledge campaign and agreed to donate at least half of their fortunes to charity. Buffett strongly feels, 'If you're in the luckiest 1% of humanity, you owe it to the rest of humanity to think about the other 99%.'[9]

Buffett also advises that one should choose their life partners wisely and always marry someone who can help one improve. Buffett was married to Susan Thompson from 1952 until her death in 2004, although the couple separated in the '70s. He and Susan have three children: Susan, Howard and

---

[8] Yeho Lucy Hwang, 'Bill Gates's and Warren Buffett's Top Advice for College Students', *Inc.*, 30 January 2017. Available at https://www.inc.com/yeho-lucy-hwang/warren-buffett-to-college-students-curiosity-can-change-your-life.html; accessed on 17 March 2021.

[9] Marcel Schwantes, 'Warren Buffett Gave This Brilliant Advice to Billionaires but It Can Instantly Improve Your Life Too', *Inc.*, 23 April 2018. Available at https://www.inc.com/marcel-schwantes/warren-buffett-gave-this-brilliant-advice-to-billionaires-but-it-can-also-improve-your-life-fast.html; accessed on 17 March 2021.

Peter. Later, after Susan's death, Buffett married his long-time partner—incidentally introduced to him by Susan herself—Astrid Menks in 2006. According to an interview with *TIME*, he would often say, 'Susie put me together and Astrid keeps me together.'[10]

Associate with the right people.

Modest and always smiling, Buffett, is in fact, very unlike the picture of a typical billionaire. He lives a rather frugal life, still staying in the same house he bought in 1957. In a 2013 *CNN* interview, he said, 'I don't throw anything away until I've had it 20 or 25 years.'[11] He once said at an annual shareholder's meeting, 'My life couldn't be happier. In fact, it'd be worse if I had six or eight houses. So, I have everything I need to have, and I don't need any more because it doesn't make a difference after a point.'[12] He doesn't shy away from being thrifty—the Lincoln Town Car even had the word on its license plate—and legend has it that once he even treated his friend Bill Gates to McDonald's using discount coupons. Warren is a huge fan of the franchise himself, often picking up his breakfast there on his way to work. Among his other favourites is Coca-Cola. In an interview with *Fortune* he said, 'I'm one quarter Coca-Cola. If I eat 2700 calories a day, a quarter of that is Coca-

---

[10]Barbara Kiviat, 'Warren Buffett Tells All: The Women in His Life', *TIME*, 23 September 2008. Available at http://content.time.com/time/business/article/0,8599,1843839,00.html; accessed on 17 March 2021.

[11]Lateef Mungin, 'Warren Buffett Opens His Wallet for Piers Morgan and America', *CNN*, 23 October 2013. Available at https://www.cnn.com/2013/10/23/us/warren-buffett-piers-interview/index.html; accessed on 17 March 2021.

[12]Brendan Matthews, 'Warren Buffett Finally Explains Why Being Cheap Leads to Happiness', *The Motley Fool*, 8 June 2016. Available at https://www.fool.com/investing/general/2014/06/08/warren-buffett-finally-explains-why-being-cheap-le.aspx; accessed on 17 March 2021.

Cola. I drink at least five 12-ounce servings.'[13] Incidentally, so happy is he with the product that he has even invested in the company in 1988 and was its director from 1989 until 2006. Today, it still forms one of Berkshire Hathaway's most lucrative investments. Buffett has a simple motto for being successful. He says, 'Rule No. 1: Never lose money. Rule No. 2: Don't forget rule No. 1.'[14]

If you want to be successful, don't lose money.

In an interview with Yahoo Finance's editor-in-chief, Buffett said, 'By far the best investment you can make is in yourself.'[15] Working on oneself brings great returns as he has himself exemplified through his life. Now a charismatic billionaire businessman, Warren used to be quite shy when he was young and admits in his biography *The Snowball: Warren Buffett and the Business of Life* by Alice Schroeder that he used to often throw up before he had to give a public speech. In order to overcome his shyness and improve his communication skills, he enrolled in a course by Dale Carnegie, which taught him confidence and communication skills that changed his life forever. Today, he shares his words of wisdom with more than 40,000 people every year at the Berkshire Hathaway annual shareholder meeting.

When a group of students at Georgia Tech had asked him how he measured success, the now 90-year-old Buffett had said, 'Basically, when you get to my age, you'll really measure

---

[13]Patricia Sellers, 'Warren Buffett's Secret to Staying Young: "I Eat Like a Six-Year-Old"', *Fortune*, 25 February 2015. Available at https://fortune.com/2015/02/25/warren-buffett-diet-coke/; accessed on 17 March 2021.
[14]https://www.youtube.com/watch?v=vCpT-UmVf3g; accessed on 17 March 2021.
[15]https://news.yahoo.com/warren-buffett-shares-keys-success-134329028.html; accessed on 17 March 2021.

your success in life by how many of the people you want to have love you actually do love you.' He also added, 'The only way to get love is to be loveable.'[16] Buffett is an epitome of a well-loved and well-respected billionaire businessman. While awarding him with the Presidential Medal of Freedom on 16 February 2011, then president of the US, Barack Obama, rightly described him as 'not only one of the world's richest men but also one of the most admired and respected' who has 'demonstrated that integrity isn't just a good trait, it is good for business.'[17]

Aim to be loved by those around you.

---

[16]Alice Schroeder, *The Snowball: Warren Buffett and the Business of Life* (2009, Bantam Books).

[17]*Reuters*, 'Obama Awards Freedom Medals to Bush, Merkel, Buffett', 16 February 2011. Available at https://www.reuters.com/article/us-obama-medals/obama-awards-freedom-medals-to-bush-merkel-buffett-idUSTRE71E60P20110215; accessed on 17 March 2021.

CONCLUSION

Now that you've finished the book, read the stories, empathized with the struggles and awed at the achievements, you are hopefully inspired and raring to go.

The millionaires you have encountered in this book are important not simply for the end goal that they have achieved but for the roads they have taken. It is not about what they have but who they are.

The stories you have read will tell you that becoming a millionaire is not only about wealth accumulation and how much money you have but it is about who you become on the journey.

So, once you close this book, think about who you are and who you want to become. Think about where you are right now and where you want to be.

What changes do you need to see in your life? What habits do you need to inculcate? What fears do you need to fight? What risks do you need to take?

You know you can do it. You can become a millionaire like them. You can do it before you turn 30 or even after.

Now, draw a blueprint for your life, write down your dreams, create the vision and pursue the passion.

You are the protagonist of your own life story. You are also the author.

So, create the story that you are proud to tell. Build the life that you want to live. Make yourself the millionaire you want to be.

Made in the USA
Monee, IL
03 May 2026